The Freshwater and Brackish Water Fish and Decapod Crustaceans of St. Vincent: An Inventory

**The Freshwater and Brackish Water Fish
and Decapod Crustaceans of St. Vincent:
An Inventory**

©2025 John Renton

Published by Hobo Jungle Press
St. Vincent & the Grenadines, W.I.
Sharon, Connecticut, USA

ISBN #979-8-9922251-0-5
Library of Congress Control Number: 2024950100
First edition
January 2025

All rights reserved. No part of this publication may be reproduced, distributed, or transmitted in any form or by any means, including photocopying, recording, or other electronic or mechanical methods, without the prior written permission of the publisher, except in the case of brief quotations embodied in critical reviews and certain other noncommercial uses permitted by copyright law.

The Freshwater and Brackish Water Fish and Decapod Crustaceans of St. Vincent: An Inventory

John Renton

Acknowledgements

The St. Vincent and the Grenadines Environment Fund (SVGEF), without whose sponsorship this project would not have been possible.

Executive Director of the SVGEF, Ms. Louise Mitchell, and Projects Coordinator of the SVGEF, Mr. Stephan Hornsey, for their support.

The Ministry of Agriculture, Forestry, Fisheries, Rural Transformation, Industry and Labour for its support.

Director of Forestry, Mr. Fitzgerald Providence, without whose support and advice this project would not have been possible.

Chief Fisheries Officer, Mrs. Jennifer Cruickshank-Howard, for her support and for provision of tritri fishery data.

Deputy Director of the National Parks, Rivers and Beaches Authority, Mrs. Rodecia Simmons-Tannis, and Communications and Public Relations Officer, Ms. Twanique Barrow, for their support.

The staff of the Forestry Department who assisted with the field survey: Mr. Ian Christopher, Mr. Quasim Roban, Mr. Romano Pierre, Mr. Maciah Farrel, Mr. Jamali Slater, and Miss Jodelia Simmons.

Mr. Shem Gaymes, river fishing expert on the survey.

Miss Alexia Burgin and Mrs. Susan Singh-Renton for data management.

Expert Fishermen who participated in the questionnaire and shared their knowledge: Mr. Kanhai Jackson, Mr. Okeitho Dellimore, Mr. Omran McMillan, Mr. Al Johnson, Mr. Chesley Nedd, Mr. Elias

Mrs. Ronique Joseph and Mr. Stephan Hornsey for project photography.

Mrs. Madeleine Smith for her illustrations of fish and shrimp.

Ms. Gabriela Hogue, Collections Manager Ichthology, North Carolina Museum of Natural Sciences, for her review of the manuscript.

The media, for coverage of the project, particularly Searchlight, NBC Radio, SVG TV, The Ministry of Agriculture Media Unit.

Fr. Mark De Silva for use of photographs and encouragement.

Mrs. Susan Singh-Renton for her support at all stages of the project.

TO CITE THIS DOCUMENT:
Renton, J. 2024. The Freshwater and Brackish Water Fish and Decapod Crustaceans of St. Vincent: An Inventory. St. Vincent & the Grenadines Environment Fund Report, svgef.org. Kingstown: Hobo Jungle Press. 132 pp.

Table of Contents

List of figures v
List of tables viii
Introduction 1
Methods 3
   FIELD SURVEY 3
      Selection and range of stations sampled 3
      Field team and fishing methods 6
      Collection of samples and data 9
   COLLECTION OF LOCAL, TRADITIONAL KNOWLEDGE - SURVEY OF RIVER FISHERS 10
Results and Discussion 12
   FRESHWATER AND BRACKISH WATER FISH 12
      Family: Anguillidae (eels) 14
      Family: Carangidae (jacks) 16
      Family: Centropomidae (snooks) 17
      Family: Cichlidae (mouth brooders) 18
      Family: Eleotridae (sleepers) 20
      Family: Gobiesocidae (Clingfish) 23
      Family: Gobiidae (gobies) 25
      Family: Haemulidae (grunts) 38
      Family: Lutjanidae (snappers) 40
      Family: Megalopidae (tarpons) 41
      Family: Mugilidae (mullets) 43
      Family: Poeciliidae (livebearers) 46
      Family: Syngnathidae (pipefish) 48
   FRESHWATER AND BRACKISH WATER DECAPOD CRUSTACEANS 51
      Infraorder Caridea – True Shrimp 51
      Family: ATYIDAE 52
      Family: XIPHOCARIDIDAE 61
      Family: PALAEMONIDAE 62
      Infraorder: Brachyura – True Crabs 75
      Family: Portunidae 76
      Family: Pseudothelphusidae 78
      Family: Grapsidae 81
   OTHER FRESHWATER TAXA OBSERVED DURING THE SURVEY 83
   THE FRESHWATER FISHERY OF ST. VINCENT 86
   PATTERNS OF BIODIVERSITY 87
      River Type 87
      Habitat Type 87
      Feeding Relationships 91
      The Freshwater and Brackish Water Fish and Decapod Diversity of St. Vincent
      Compared to Other Islands in the region 92
      An Overview of the IUCN Conservation Status of Species Recorded in the St. Vincent Survey 93
      Why No Endemic Freshwater Fish from St. Vincent? 94
   THREATS TO FRESHWATER BIODIVERSITY IN ST. VINCENT 95
      Volcanic Eruption 95
      Flow Modification 97
      River Engineering 99
      Climate Change 101
      Pollution 103
      Invasive Species 103
      Exploitation by Fisheries 104

 A Habitat under Threat – The Semi-Estuarine Pool... *107*
 The Institutional and Legal Mechanisms for the Conservation of Freshwater Biodiversity in St. Vincent and the Grenadines... *108*

Conclusions **110**

Bibliography **111**

APPENDIX 1. TECHNICAL TERMS AND MEASUREMENTS **129**

APPENDIX 2. RIVER FISHERS' QUESTIONNAIRE **131**

List of figures

Figure 1. Map of stations sampled. 3

Figure 2. Examples of habitat types sampled during the survey. 7

Figure 3. Fishing gear utilized during the survey. 8

Figure 4. Sorting, measuring and recording on site. 9

Figure 5. Identification of specimens with the aid of a microscope and dichotomous keys. 9

Figure 6. Map of the location of the residence of river fishermen who participated in the survey. 10

Figure 7. Some of the fishermen who participated in the interviews. 11

Figure 8. *Anguilla rostrata*, yellow eel phase, captured from the Petite Bordel River, St. Vincent. 14

Figure 9. *Caranx latus*. 16

Figure 10. *Centropomus undecimalis*. 17

Figure 11. *Oreochromis mossambicus*, male, captured in the Buccament River. 19

Figure 12. *Eleotris perniger*. 20

Figure 13. *Gobiomorus dormitor*. 22

Figure 14. *Gobiesox cephalus* (i) dorsal view (ii) ventral view showing sucking disk. 24

Figure 15. *Awaous banana*. (i) *Awaous banana* adult with enlarged cheek. (ii) Ventral view showing fused pelvic fins forming a disk. 25

Figure 16. *Sicydium spp.* from the Colonaire River. 27

Figure 17. *Sicydium* goby, ventral view showing fused pelvic fins forming a disk. 28

Figure 18. Urogenital Papilla of *Sicydium* gobies (a) male (b) female. 28

Figure 19. The Lifecycle of Sicydium gobies. 29

Figure 20. (i) Newly run post-larval *Sicydium*. (ii) Juvenile *Sicydium* after 3 days in fresh water. 30

Figure 21. St. Vincent monthly average rainfall and Tritri landings 1998-2007. Data from St.Vincent Fisheries Division. ...31

Figure 22. Tritri Fishing Methods. (i) Tritri traps in the Richmond River, 2022. (ii) Lifting tritri traps in the Buccament River, 2001. (iii) The flambeau method of tritri fishing. (iv) The seine method of tritri fishing. 32

Figure 23. Vincentian Postage Stamp, depicting Tritri. 33

Figure 24. *Sicydium plumieri*. 33

Figure 25. Upper jaw dentition of *Sicydium plumieri*, consisting of two rows of unicuspid teeth. 34

Figure 26. The "Pretty macack". 35

Figure 27. *Sicydium punctatum*. (i) Specimen identified to species level by dentition (ii) Photograph taken 1st July believed to be a male in nuptial colouration. 36

Figure 28. Tricuspid upper jaw teeth of *Sicydium punctatum*. 36

Figure 29. *Sicydium buscki*, unicuspid upper jaw dentition. 37

Figure 30. *Rhonciscus crocro*, captured from the Wallibou River, March 2023. 39

Figure 31. *Lutjanus jocu*. 40

Figure 32. Juvenile *Megalops atlanticus* captured from the semi-estuarine pool of the Buccament River. 41

Figure 33. *Dajaus monticola*. 43

Figure 34. Hook and line fishing for *Dajaus monticola* in the Yambou River. 44

Figure 35. *Mugil curema*. 45

Figure 36. A wild-caught male *Poecilia reticulata*. 46

Figure 37. *Microphis lineatus*. (i) Specimens showing head. (ii) A ventral view of a section of the brood pouch of a male containing eggs. 49

Figure 38. *Atya innocous*. 52

Figure 39. Illustration of *Atya innocous* male. 53

Figure 40. *Atya innocous* filter feeding facing into the current. 54

Figure 41. (i) A traditional crayfish basket. (ii) A catch of bookies. 55

Figure 42. Male *Atya scabra*. 56

Figure 43. *Micratya poeyi*. 57

Figure 44. Dorsal Rostral teeth of *Micratya poeyi*. 58

Figure 45. Illustration of the colour patterns in *Micratya poeyi*. 58

Figure 46. Illustration of *Jonga serri*. 59

Figure 47. Ventral rostral teeth in *Jonga serrei*. 60

Figure 48. *Xiphocaris elongata*. 61

Figure 49. *Macrobrachium acanthurus*. 63

Figure 50. *Macrobrachium carcinus* Adult male. 65

Figure 51. Teeth on the cutting edge of the finger of the second pereiopod of *M. carcinus*. 65

Figure 52. Juvenile *M. carcinus* with prominent longitudinal stripes. 66

Figure 53. A river lobster captured at the semi-estuarine pool of the Buccament River (station 26) by expert river fisherman, Shem Gaymes using a spear gun he made himself. 67

Figure 54. Specialised hook and line method used to catch *Macrobrachium carcinus*, river lobster. 68

Figure 55. *Macrobrachium crenulatum* male. 69

Figure 56. Illustration of *M. crenulatum*. 69

Figure 57. *Macrobrachium faustinum* male. 71

Figure 58. Illustration of *Macrobrachium heterochirus*, male. 73

Figure 59. *Macrobrachium heterochirus*, male. 73

Figure 60. *Callinectes sapidus*, male. 76

Figure 61. Ventral view of a male *C. sapidus* showing first pleopods. 77

Figure 62. Ventral view of a female *C. sapidus* with a wide apron and orange pincers. 77

Figure 63. *Guinotia dentata*. 79

Figure 64. Ventral view of a female *Guinotia dentata*. 79

Figure 65. Ventral view of a male *Guinotia dentata*. 80

Figure 66. Dorsal view, *Armases roberti*. 81

Figure 67. Anterior view, *Armases roberti*, showing orange fingers of chelipeds. 82

Figure 68. *Nereina punctulata*. 85

Figure 69. *Ferrissia irrorata*. 85

Figure 70. *Melanoides tuberculata*. 85

Figure 71. Trends in fish species occurrence in three major habitats. 88

Figure 72. Trends in shrimp species occurrence in three major habits. 88

Figure 73. Fish species occurrence, according to location within the river system. 90

Figure 74. Decapod crustacean occurrence, according to location within the river system. 90

Figure 75. The food web of a Caribbean Stream, Grande-Anse, Guadeloupe. 91

Figure 76. *Dormitator maculatus*, caught in the semi-estuarine pool of the Buccament River, 2007. 92

Figure 77. Wallibou River on 13th April 2021 after a pyroclastic flow. 96

Figure 78. Wallibou River December 2021. 97

Figure 79. Wallibou River, Station 40, March 2023.. 97

Figure 80. The Richmond River below the intake of the hydro plant during the dry season. 98

Figure 81. Channel alteration made at the lower Buccament River in April 2022. 100

Figure 82. Hydroelectric dam on the Cumberland River at Spring Village. 100

Figure 83. The Buccament River, Vermont, on 11th January 2014, showing erosion of the bank and scouring of the riverbed caused by the 2013 Christmas Eve Flood. 101

List of tables

Table 1. Survey stations mapped in Figure 1. River and habitat classifications after Harrison and Rankin (1976a). 4

Table 2. Classification of the rivers of St. Vincent after Harrison and Rankin (1976a). 5

Table 3. Classification of Fluvial Habitats after Harrison and Rankin (1976a) 5

Table 4. Fish species identified during the survey. 13

Table 5. An inventory of shrimp species identified during the survey. 51

Table 6. An inventory of crab species identified during the survey. 75

Table 7. An inventory of mollusc species identified during the survey. 84

Table 8. An inventory of amphibian species identified during the survey..84

Table 9. Summary of the findings of the survey of river fishers. 86

Table 10. Results of χ^2 Tests to investigate the association between frequency of occurrence of fish and decapod crustacean species and river type. 87

Table 11. The results of χ^2 Tests to investigate the association between frequency of occurrence of fish and decapod crustacean species and habitat type. 87

Table 12. Summary of the IUCN global conservation status of the species recorded in the St. Vincent Survey. 93

Introduction

St. Vincent and the Grenadines (13° 15' N, 61° 12' W) is composed of 30 islands and keys and is part of the Windward Islands chain of the Lesser Antilles in the Caribbean Sea. St. Vincent is the largest island in the state, with a land area of 303 km^2, which accounts for 78% of the total land area of the State.

St. Vincent has a maritime tropical climate with temperatures ranging from 24° to 31°C and an annual rainfall of 2000 mm and 4000 mm at low and high elevations respectively. The wet season occurs between June and November when rainfall averages 200 mm per month. The dry season occurs between December and May. Relative to the annual average, temperatures are generally 2°C cooler between December and March (World Bank Group, 2024).

The island is of volcanic in origin. The northern third is dominated by the La Soufriere volcano (1220m in elevation), which last erupted in April 2021. Jagged, forested mountain peaks form the central part of the island. Most of the land is steeply sloping.

Drainage is composed of rivers with high gradients and maximum course of 10 km. Rivers typically flow through steeply sloping valleys and are torrential in nature all the way to the sea. Some rivers have a small alluvial plain in the lower reaches. Waterfalls are common in the upper reaches. Mean water temperatures range from 27.6°C at sea level to 22.25°C at 452 m above sea level with a 3°C diurnal variation. There is little seasonal variation in water temperature. Dissolved oxygen is typically 80-90% saturation (Harrison and Rankin, 1976a).

Numerous dry rivers or bournes occur on the slopes of La Soufriere. These increased in number due to the 2021 eruption when several river valleys, which previously contained flowing streams, became filled with loose tephra. The small Crater Lake created by this eruption is the only natural body of standing water in St. Vincent. There are no permanent rivers in the Grenadine islands due to their small land areas and dry climate.

The freshwater biodiversity of St. Vincent, and of the Eastern Caribbean in general, is poorly described. To date, no comprehensive lists of freshwater and brackish water fish and decapod crustacean species of St. Vincent have been published. The lack of published scientific literature has also contributed to the freshwater biodiversity being overlooked in respect of water resource management. The most significant academic contributions to the scientific description of the freshwaters of St. Vincent were done by Harrison and Rankin (1976a, 1976b). These studies described "the freshwater habitats and water quality" and "fauna of its running waters". These studies provided a detailed description of the invertebrate fauna found in different habitats within the rivers, but fish were not included.

Consequently, there is little information in the literature regarding the freshwater and brackish water fish fauna of St. Vincent. The Country Environmental Profile for St. Vincent and the Grenadines (Caribbean Conservation Association, 1991) states that "The country's freshwater fishes, comprising several species of gobies, mountain mullets, clingfish, etc., are not well studied." The status of knowledge remains the same to date. The study of freshwater fish biodiversity in the Lesser Antilles has also been hindered because the taxonomy of some of the major regional freshwater fish taxa was unresolved for a long time. Publication of reviews of the Spiny Cheek Sleepers, Genus *Eleotris* (Pezold and Gage, 2002) and the *Sicydium* gobies (Watson, 2000) has made identification of species in these taxa now possible.

In comparison, decapod crustaceans, freshwater shrimp (local name "crayfish") and freshwater crabs are significant components of St. Vincent's fluvial ecology and are better described in the literature. Although no comprehensive list of decapod crustaceans found in St. Vincent exists to date, fragmentary records can be found in the literature. An early record of the habitat of the shrimps *Atya scabra* and *Palaemon carcinus* (synonym for *Macrobrachium carcinus*) from St. Vincent was recorded in the Transactions of the Linnean Society (Reverent Lansdown Guilding, 1824). Chance and Hobbs (1969) examined museum specimens from the region and noted four species of freshwater and brackish water shrimp and one crab collected in St. Vincent. Harrison and Rankin (1976a, 1976b) reported four additional species and three crab species. From these sources a total of nine species of shrimp in three families and two species of crab in two families are recorded in the literature for St. Vincent. They are: Shrimp - Family Atyidae (*Atya innocous, Atya scabra, Jonga serrei, Micratya poeyi*) Family Xphocarididae (*Xiphocaris elongata*), Family Palaemonidea (*Macrobrachium acanthurus, Macrobrachium carcinus, Macrobrachium faustinum, Macrobrachium heterochrius*); Crabs - Family Potamocarcinidae (*Guinotia dentata*), Family Grapsidae (*Armases roberti*).

Sporadic museum collections of freshwater fish and decapod crustacean specimens from St. Vincent are lodged in museums in the United Kingdom, United States of America and Europe. These collections were usually made by visiting zoologists. One of the earliest and most extensive collections was made by H.H. Smith, a professional naturalist who was commissioned by the Royal Society to collect specimens from the Windward Islands during 1889-1895 (Wikipedia, 2024). His collection from St. Vincent includes the following eight species: American eel (*Anguilla rostrata*), Large scale spiny cheek sleeper (*Eleotris pisonis*), Bigmouth sleeper (*Gobiomorus dormitor*), Riverine clingfish (*Gobiesox* cephalus), Plumier's stone biting goby (*Sicydium plumieri*), Riverine goby (*Awawous banana*), Mountain mullet (*Dajaus monticola*), and Burro grunt (*Rhonciscus crocro*). These specimens are deposited in the Natural History Museum in London. No review of museum specimens captured from freshwater and brackish water environments in St. Vincent has been undertaken.

For generations, the population of St. Vincent has exploited "crayfish", crabs and river fish as a source of sustenance. A wealth of informal information regarding the freshwater fish and fisheries resides with persons who participate in traditional river fishing. River fishermen possess a vast store of local, traditional knowledge regarding freshwater fish, particularly their habitats, how to catch them and the status of these resources. There has been no previous attempt to make a written record of this local, traditional knowledge.

Methods

Field Survey

A field survey, to identify and record the occurrence the of freshwater and brackish water fish and decapod crustaceans present in St. Vincent W.I., was carried out between 29th January and 7th June 2023.

Selection and range of stations sampled

A total of 40 stations in 14 river systems were sampled (Figure 1, Table 1). River, habitat, and location details for each of the 40 stations are provided in Table 1. Rivers sampled were classified according to the criteria established by Harrison and Rankin (1976a) (Table 2). Sample stations were also categorised according to the fluvial habitats, as described by Harrison and Rankin (1976a) and noted in Table 3. Examples of the major habitat types are depicted in Figure 2. The present survey did not include the Grenadines although some temporary streams in Bequia and Union Island are reported to contain shrimp and fish (Fr. Mark DaSilva, personal communication, 2023). These temporary streams should be surveyed in a subsequent study.

Figure 1. Map of stations sampled.

Table 1. Survey stations mapped in Figure 1. River and habitat classifications after Harrison and Rankin (1976a).

	Station	River Type	Habitat Type	Latitude (N)	Longitude (W)	Altitude (m)
1	Fancy River Nr. Intake	Minor River	Mountain Torrent	13.369747	-61.139691	181
2	Kramaku River Nr. Owia above highway	Minor River	Mountain Torrent	13.406220	-61.107650	33
3	Rabbaca River Nr. Hydrothermal site	Bourne	Mountain Torrent	13.308860	-61.148770	255
4	Grand Sable River, river mouth	Minor River	Semi-estuarine	13.266130	-61.117430	<8
5	Grand Sable River below confluence	Minor River	Foothill Torrent	13.267610	-61.127490	53
6	Grand Sable River Congo Valley below falls	Minor River	Mountain Torrent	13.271780	-61.144970	217
7	Grand Sable River Congo Valley above falls	Minor River	Mountain Torrent	13.271736	-61.145253	231
8	Colonaire River mouth	Major River	Semi-estuarine	13.240110	-61.116440	<8
9	Colonaire River SDA Church	Major River	Foothill Torrent	13.242780	-61.123430	34
10	Colonaire River Three Rivers Bridge	Major River	Foothill Torrent	13.246817	-61.136156	80
11	Colonaire River River 14	Major River	Mountain Torrent	13.250010	-61.146890	143
12	Colonaire River below hydro intake	Major River	Mountain Torrent	13.241721	-61.158000	207
13	Camacarbou River mouth	Stream	Semi-estuarine	13.221820	-61.126500	<8
14	Camacarbou River lower	Stream	Foothill Torrent	13.224760	-61.132380	44
15	Camacarbou New Adelphi below falls	Stream	Mountain Torrent	13.228800	-61.138956	100
16	Camacarbou New Adelphi above falls	Stream	Mountain Torrent	13.228619	-61.139514	107
17	Spring Biabou mouth	Stream	Semi-estuarine	13.185080	-61.141740	<8
18	Yambou River mouth	Major River	Semi-estuarine	13.164210	-61.143780	<8
19	Yambou River above Windward Highway	Major River	Foothill Torrent	13.169210	-61.149360	29
20	Teviot River Montreal back rd. bridge	Major River	Mountain Torrent	13.203250	-61.182170	403
21	Teviot River nr. Catchment	Major River	Mountain Torrent	13.209331	-61.189344	486
22	Canash	Rivulet	Stream	13.125830	-61.189470	<8
23	Warrawarro River Mouth Arnos Vale	Minor River	Semi-estuarine	13.140560	-61.211320	<8
24	Warrawarro River nr. spa	Minor River	Mountain torrent	13.162704	-61.192629	118
25	Warrawwaro River Fenton above bridge	Minor River	Mountain torrent	13.186930	-61.206660	380
26	Buccament River Mouth	Major River	Semi-estuarine	13.191860	-61.267100	<8
27	Buccament River Playing Field	Major River	Foothill Torrent	13.192858	-61.263940	<8
28	Buccament River Above Playing Field	Major River	Foothill Torrent	13.193270	-61.259310	15
29	Buccament River Vermont nr Nature Trail	Major River	Mountain Torrent	13.212726	-61.216309	256
30	Wallilabou River mouth	Minor River	Semi-estuarine	13.248490	-61.270300	<8
31	Wallilabou River above Heritage Centre	Minor River	Foothill Torrent	13.247560	-61.259550	64
32	Cumberland River Mouth	Major River	Semi-Estuarine	13.265340	-61.259740	<8
33	Cumberland River below Hydro "let out"	Major River	Foothill Torrent	13.264370	-61.257440	14
34	Cumberland River Hermitage	Major River	Mountain Torrent	13.247810	-61.212840	360
35	Petit Bordel River mouth	Minor River	Semi-Estuarine	13.289100	-61.246880	<8
36	Petit bordel River top of village	Minor River	Mountain Torrent	13.284300	-61.244720	46
37	Richmond River mouth	Major River	Semi-estuarine	13.308120	-61.234910	<8
38	Richmond River trib. below Darkview Falls	Major River	Mountain Torrent	13.291292	-61.221920	108
39	Richmond River Ever Green	Major River	Mountain Torrent	13.290700	-61.221870	115
40	Wallibou River Lower	Major River	Foothill Torrent	13.312960	-61.230060	22

Table 2. Classification of the rivers of St. Vincent after Harrison and Rankin (1976a).

River Classification	Altitude of Origin
Major Rivers	Larger rivers. Originate in the high peaks with a mean altitude at origin of 884m. Reach the sea within 7-10km.
Minor Rivers	Smaller rivers with altitude of origin between 610 and 475m. Reach the sea within 4 -6km.
Stream High Level	Originate in foothills between 610 and 305m. May be tributaries or remain distinct.
Stream Low Level	Originate in foothills between 305 and 152m. May be tributaries or remain distinct.
Rivulets	Very small, short watercourses found on the windward and south coasts. Originate between 91 and 31m.
Bourne	Bournes or "dry rivers" originate at a range of altitudes between 1219 and 305m

Table 3. Classification of Fluvial Habitats after Harrison and Rankin (1976a)

Habitat Type	Flow Characteristics	Description
Mountain torrent zone	Fast Flow	<ul><li>Torrential</li><li>Rocky bed</li><li>Small waterfalls and cascades. Infrequent pools</li><li>Often flow through rainforest or secondary forest</li><li>Tree roots occasionally trail in the water</li><li>Leaf pack often found between stones</li><li>Stones appear clean however are coated with a film of diatoms</li><li>Runs clear except after very heavy rain</li></ul>
Foothill torrent zone	Fast Flow	<ul><li>Mountain torrents unite to form foothill torrents</li><li>Run through agricultural and human settlement</li><li>Valleys steep sided.</li><li>Cascades are reduced, runs and riffles numerous; common substrate boulders and cobble.</li><li>Pools are numerous, substrate cobble, sand and occasionally mud</li><li>Leaf pack is less common than in mountain torrents</li><li>Stones are discoloured by diatom growth</li><li>Tufts of filamentous algae are found on stones in areas of agriculture and human settlement</li></ul>
Stream	Moderate-flow	<ul><li>Originate in secondary peaks</li><li>Many flow directly to the sea, some are tributaries</li><li>Run through agriculture and human settlement</li><li>Upper reaches torrential with cascades and riffles</li><li>Pools often with sand substrate</li></ul>
Rivulet	Slow-flow	<ul><li>Arise in agricultural and settled areas or dry scrub</li><li>Short in length</li><li>Small watercourses</li></ul>
Semi-estuarine pool	Variable flow. Those with a sand bar impeding exit	<ul><li>Not true estuaries as they are not tidal</li><li>The pool is formed when the rivers exit to the sea is dammed by a sand bar of beach sand</li><li>Salinity is variable. Under normal conditions salinities in leeward rivers are 10-14 $^0/_{00}$ at the seaward side of the bar, 2-4</li></ul>

Habitat Type	Flow Characteristics	Description
	to the sea have slow-flow.	$^0/_{00}$ on the landward side of the bar and 0 $^0/_{00}$ 5m behind the bar. Floods which break through the sand bar and storm surge which crests the sand bar impact salinity in this pool • Substrate is variable. Some are stony others sand and silt • Often fringed by emergent grasses
Bourne or "dry river"	Temporary	• Flow to the sea only during heavy spate • Mostly occur on the slopes of the La Soufriere volcano • Some flow strongly in the upper reaches with the stream lost into loose volcanic tephra in the middle or lower reaches

Field team and fishing methods

Members of the Forestry Department and an expert river fisherman assisted in the collection of specimens. A range of fishing gear was utilized according to the nature of the habitat sampled (Figure 3).

Fishing gear included –
(i) A seine net, 10 ft long with 3/8 in knotless mesh. This net was deployed in pools with sandy substrate. The seine was also held fast against emergent vegetation to capture fish that were using the vegetation as cover.
(ii) Dip nets with 3/8 in mesh. Dip nets were worked in emergent vegetation, trailing tree roots, and accumulations of leaves (leaf pack). 'Kick' samples were taken when the substrate was composed of small stones.
(iii) A cast net 5 ft in diameter with 3/8 in mesh.
(iv) The expert fisherman used a diving glass for fishing. Fish and shrimp were caught by hand while wearing a protective glove. A spear gun was also used to shoot fish and shrimp.

(i)

(ii)

(iii)

Figure 2. Examples of habitat types sampled during the survey. (i) Semi-estuarine pool in the Buccament River, Station 26. (ii) Foothill torrent in the Colonaire River, Station 9. (iii) Mountain torrent on the Cumberland River, Station 34.

Figure 3. Fishing gear utilized during the survey. **(i)** Seine worked against emergent vegetation. **(ii)** Seine used in a pool with sandy substrate. **(iii)** Dip net worked in trailing tree roots. **(iv)** Cast net. **(v)** Diving glass and spear gun.

Collection of samples and data

All specimens collected were sorted on site (Figure 4). Species that could be identified immediately were measured (see Appendix 1 for morphometric measurements taken) and returned to the river in live condition. Where specimens could not be identified on site, they were collected and identified later with the aid of a microscope and an appropriate dichotomous key (Figure 5). For voucher specimens of the species recorded, these were retained and preserved in 84.5% ethanol, to be permanently vouchered at the North Carolina Museum of Natural Sciences in Raleigh, North Carolina, United State of America. The occurrence of organisms that were observed but not captured at any station were recorded to lowest taxonomic level possible. The physical and ecological characteristics of each sample station were recorded.

Figure 4. Sorting, measuring and recording on site.

Figure 5. Identification of specimens with the aid of a microscope and dichotomous keys.

Collection of Local, Traditional Knowledge - Survey of River Fishers

Eight expert fishermen, operating in diverse locations across the sampled area (Figure 6) were identified. The aim was to collect and document local, traditional information on the descriptive characteristics of the river fishery (Figure 7). Each fisherman participated in a structured interview and a questionnaire (Appendix 2 designed to collect information regarding: their reasons for fishing, the economic value of river species, observations regarding the health of the riverine environment, vernacular names of river fish and crayfish, and fishing methods used.

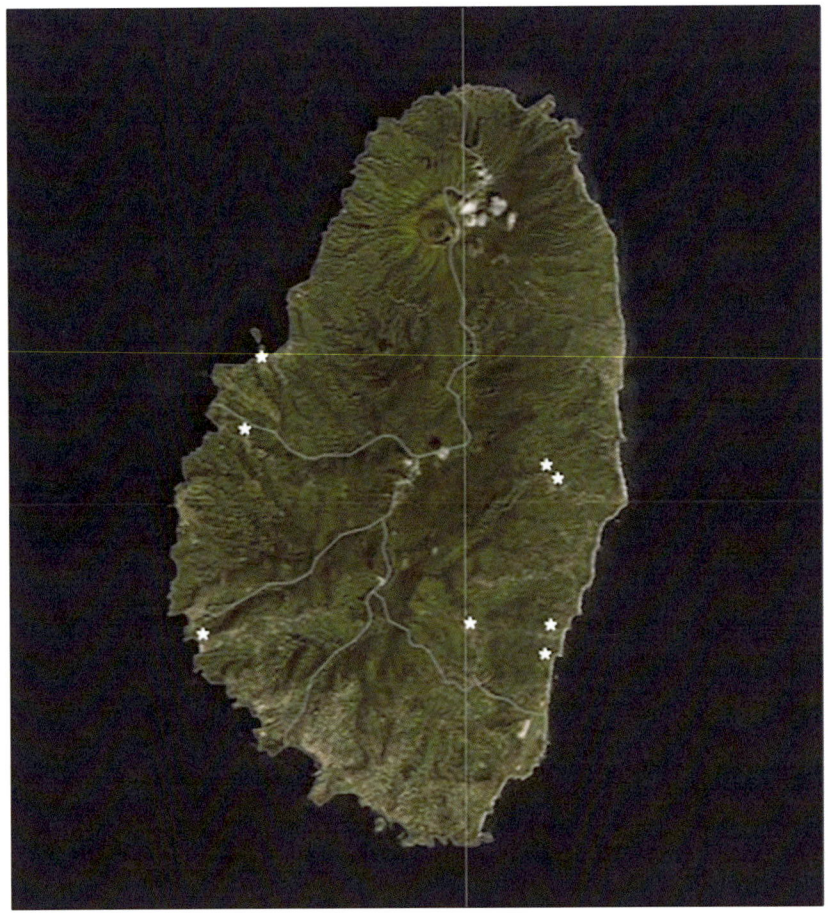

Figure 6. Map of the location of the residence of river fishermen who participated in the survey.

(i)

(ii)

(iii)

Figure 7. Some of the fishermen who participated in the interviews. (i) Mr. Chessley Nedd "Cat" of Richland Park. (ii) Mr. Shem Gaymes of Buccament Bay. (iii) Mr. Derick DeBique of Petit Bordel (seated at right) with interviewer, John Renton (seated at left).

Results and Discussion

Anatomical structures referred to in the text are shown in Appendix 1.

Freshwater and Brackish Water Fish

An inventory of freshwater and brackish water fish species recorded in the survey, with occurrence details, is given in Table 4. For each of these species, the status of the knowledge of species biology and ecology is also provided.

Table 4. Fish species identified during the survey.

Scientific Name	Vernacular Names	Common Name (Fishbase)	St. Vincent Stations Where Sp. Recorded	Number of Stations Where Sp. Occurred
Family: Anguillae (eels)				
Anguilla rostrata	Eel	American Eel	8	1
Family: Carangidae (jacks)				
Carannx latus	Crevalle	Horse-eye Jack	33	1
Family: Centropomidae				
Centropomus undecimalis		Common Snook	26	1
Family: Cichlidae				
Oreochromis niloticus	Chinee Fish	Nile tilapia	26	1
Family: Elotridae (sleepers)				
Eleotris perniger	Mud Fish	Small Scaled Spiny Cheek Sleeper	4,5,8,13,18,23,26, 30,32,35,37	11
Gobiomorus dormitor	Grouper	Bigmouth Sleeper	23,26,27,28,30,32, 35,37	8
Family: Gobiesocidae (cling fish)				
Gobiesox cephalus	Suckstone	Riverine Clingfish	8,9,27,33,35,37	6
Family: Gobiidae (gobies)				
Awaous banana	Sandfish (small) Plufjaw (large)	River Goby	8,19,23,26,28,30, 32,35,37	9
Sicydium plumieri	Macack	Plumier's Stone Biting Goby	1,2,5,7,8,9,10,12, 18,19,27,29,39	13
Sicydium punctatum	Macack	Spotted Algae Eating Goby	12	1
Sicydium buscki	Macack	Busck's Stone Biting Goby	8,9,12,19	4
Sicydium (not identified to sp.)	Macack		1,2,4-15,18-21,24 25,27,28,29,31-34,36,37,39,40	32
Family: Haemulidae (grunts)				
Rhonciscus crocro	Crocro	Burro Grunt	4,6,18,23,26,28, 32,33,35,37,40	11
Family: Lutjanidae (snappers)				
Lutjanus jocu	River snapper	Dog snapper	18,32	2
Family: Megalopidae (tarpons)				
Megalops atlanticus	River bass	Tarpon	26	1
Family: Mugilidae (mullets)				
Dajaus monticola	Mountain Mullet	Mountain Mullet	4-6,8-15,18,19,23 24,26,30,32,33, 35-37, 39,40	24
Mugil curema	Shit boatswain, Boatswain	White Mullet	8,23,26,32,37	5
Family: Poeciliidae (livebearers)				
Poecilia reticulata	Millions	Guppy	20,21	2
Family: Syngnathidae (pipe fish)				
Microphis lineatus	Tritri pilot Tritri leader	Opossum Pipefish	26,30,32,35	4

Family: Anguillidae (eels)

Anguilla rostrata (Lesueur, 1817)

COMMON NAME: American Eel

VINCENTIAN NAME: Eel

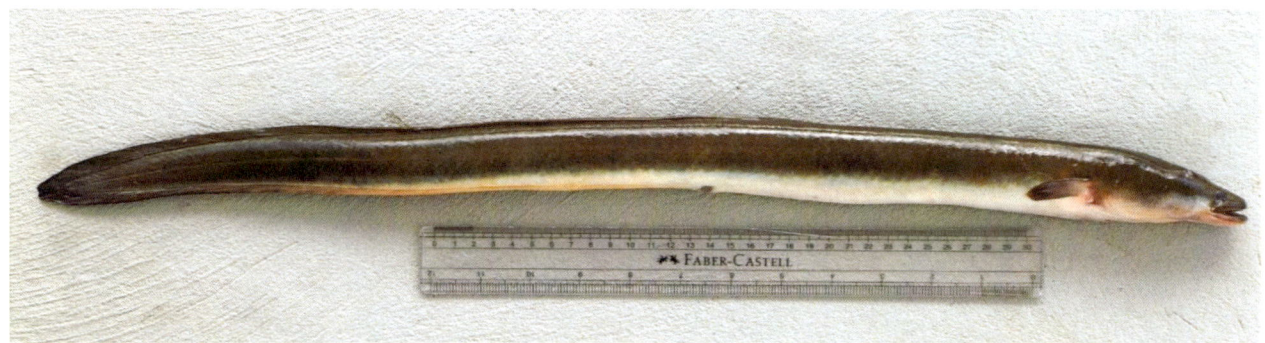

Figure 8. *Anguilla rostrata*, yellow eel phase, captured from the Petite Bordel River, St. Vincent.

STATUS: Native

RECORDED IN LITERATURE FOR ST. VINCENT: Froese and Pauly (2024)

OCCURRENCE IN THE ST. VINCENT SURVEY: Eels were captured at only one station, Station 8 at the mouth of the Colonarie River. Four small yellow eels were observed, and one was captured (120 mm total length (TL)). This species may be underrepresented in the survey due to selectivity of the fishing gear used and surveying during the day. Eels are thought to be more active at night.

DESCRIPTION: Body elongated and cylindrical and snake like (Figure 8). Dorsal and anal fins are joined and form one continuous fin around the tail. Pelvic fins are absent. Pectoral fins are conspicuous. A gill slit is located in front of the pectoral fin. Scales are very small and embedded in the skin. The fish exudes a layer of slime all over its body.
Colouration in immature fish, called yellow eels, is yellow/green on the upper surface and paler below. Sexually mature adults, called silver eels, have a black upper surface and a silver or bronze lower surface. Maximum length approximately 150 cm. Females grow larger than males. (Smith, 2002).

RANGE: North American Atlantic drainage from Greenland to Mexico, and the Greater and Lesser Antilles south to Venezuela. Most common in the Atlantic USA and southern Canada. (Jacoby *et al.*, 2017)

HABITAT: In the St. Vincent survey, small yellow eels were observed from amongst emergent grasses 200 m from the river mouth. Local fishermen, who were interviewed, reported that eels were present in most rivers, but distribution is patchy.

The American eel is tolerant of a very wide range of conditions. Jacoby *et al.* (2017) quotes Helfman *et al.* (1987) as saying that "The American Eel is thought to occupy the broadest range of habitats of any fish in the world". A study in Puerto Rico (Kwak *et al.*, 2019) found eels in a wide range of habitats including: high elevation, high gradient, clear streams; coastal slow-flowing, turbid streams;

and streams flowing through urban areas. Higher densities of smaller eels were found in the lower reaches while lower densities of larger individuals were found at higher elevations. Coat *et al.* (2011) state that the preferred habitat in the rivers of the French W.I. are clam habitats with rock crevices, a current velocity of 6cm/s and depth of 48cm.

FEEDING AND DIET: A wide range of prey is eaten, including insect larvae, aquatic invertebrates and fish (Froese and Pauly, 2024). Examination of stomach contents from eels living in rivers in New Jersey found that the diet of smaller eels (<40cm) was largely composed of aquatic insects, while that of larger eels (>40cm) was mostly composed of fish and crustaceans (Ogden, 1970).

LIFE CYCLE AND REPRODUCTION: Eels have a facultative, catadromous life cycle (Jacoby *et al.*, 2017). Many spend the majority of their lives in freshwater, but they migrate to the sea to spawn. Others spend most of their lives in brackish, estuarine habitat before migrating to the ocean to spawn. The life cycle is complex and involves several stages and habits, as follows.
1. Eggs - Females can release 0.5-4 million eggs that are 1.1 mm in diameter each. These hatch within one week.
2. Leptocephali (larvae) - Transparent leaf like larval form migrates in the upper 350m of the ocean towards the continental or island shelf. This journey lasts 7-12 months.
3. Glass Eels - Leptocephali metamorphose into the juvenile form known as glass eels when they reach a length of 55-65 mm. Glass eels are transparent but develop an elongated shape similar to the adult.
4. Elvers - As the glass eels migrate into brackish and freshwater they become pigmented and are known as elvers.
5. Yellow Eel - The majority of their life cycle is spent as a yellow eel which is the sexually immature adult phase. Yellow eels are found in freshwater and brackish environments. This life phase lasts between 3 and 20 years.
6. Silver Eel - Yellow eels develop into sexually mature adults called silver eels. Silver eels migrate from fresh and brackish waters into the ocean and onwards to the Sargasso Sea to spawn. Several physical and physiological changes take place to adapt them for migration in saltwater at depth and the digestive system degenerates. On reaching the Sargasso Sea eels from the entire range spawn. Adults are believed to die after spawning.

CONSERVATION STATUS (IUCN): Classified as Endangered by the IUCN (Casselman *et al.*, 2023). This classification was given because American eels are very likely to become extinct in their known native ranges in the near future. The reason is because of the rapid reduction in historically abundant yellow eel populations which have declined by 50-60% over three generations (Casselman *et al.*, 2023).
Eels are subjected to exploitation as yellow eels and as glass eels. Yellow eels, silver eels and elvers are considered delicacies and command high prices internationally. It is not possible to breed eels in captivity. Glass eels, caught in the wild in the USA and Canada, are exported and grown on in Asian fish farms. High demand has resulted in high prices. A brief search for American eel for sale on the internet (September 2023), yielded the following supply and price details: Maine smoked eel sell at $21.95 US for 4oz and live glass eels originating from Maine sell to Asian fish farms for $2000USD/lb. The American eel has not been listed in the USA as an endangered species and is not included in any global trade treaty, for example CITES, that prevents the species from being traded internationally. Until the species receives greater legislative protection, market forces are likely to continue to drive over-exploitation of this species.
Other environmental stressors negatively impacting the American eel include, climate change, habitat loss, habitat alteration for example dam construction, destruction of eels as they pass through hydroelectric turbines on migration, an exotic nematode parasite *Angillicola crassus* and chemical pollution.

American eels from their entire geographical distribution reproduce in one location, and hence decline in the number of spawning adults will result in reduced recruitment over the entire range including St. Vincent. Fishermen surveyed in St. Vincent all reported a decline in numbers of this species.

FISHERIES: Yellow and silver eels are targeted by fishermen in St. Vincent. Most frequently, a baited set line is left overnight to catch eels. Other methods include shooting with a spear gun and fishing by hand. Most eel fishing takes place at night.
In the region, historical commercial fisheries for eels are reported from Cuba, Dominican Republic Mexico and Puerto Rico, and glass eels from Cuba, the Dominican Republic, Haiti and Jamaica. However, the absence of recent records suggests a decline in regional eel fishing (Benchetrit and McCleave, 2015).

Family: Carangidae (jacks)

Caranx latus Agassiz, 1831

COMMON NAME: Horse Eye Jack

VINCENTIAN NAME: Crevalle

Figure 9. *Caranx latus*.

STATUS: Native

RECORDED IN LITERATURE FOR ST. VINCENT: Froese and Pauly (2024)

OCCURRENCE IN THE ST. VINCENT SURVEY: One specimen recorded from station 33, the lower reaches of the Cumberland River.

DESCRIPTION: Body deep 2.8-3.2 times fork length, 19-21 dorsal fin rays, 32-39 scutes, 16-19 gill rakers on lower limb of fist gill arch. No oval dark spot on pectoral fin. Maximum size 80 cm fork length (Cervigón *et al.*, 1993). One juvenile, with fork length 55.1 mm, was recorded in the present survey (Figure 9).

RANGE: Both sides of the Atlantic: from New Jersey to Rio de Janeiro Brazil and the Caribbean in the Western Atlantic Smith-Vaniz (2002).

HABITAT: The station where the specimen was found was a foot hill torrent located at 300 m from the river mouth and at an elevation of 14 m. The water at this location is fresh.
This species is predominantly marine. However, Guazzelli *et al.* (2021) recorded juveniles in euryhaline habitats in Brazil. The species is known to enter freshwater (Robertson and Van Tassell, 2023).

FEEDING AND DIET: Analysis of stomach contents of *C. latus* from an estuarine environment in Brazil found fish, mostly gobies, to be the most frequently occurring items in the diet, followed by crustaceans (Guazzelli *et al.*, 2021).

LIFE CYCLE AND REPRODUCTION: Reproduction occurs in marine habitats. Paired courtship within schools of 1000 fish take place at the point of reef drop off. Spawning is synchronised with the lunar cycle and occurs in the week after the full moon between the months of February and April according to a study carried out in Belize (Graham and Castellanos, 2005).

CONSERVATION STATUS (IUCN): Not evaluated.

IMPORTANCE TO FISHERIES: Not targeted by river fishermen in St. Vincent.
There are significant marine fisheries for this species in Brazil (Gonzales *et al.*, 2022).

Family: Centropomidae (snooks)

Centropomus undecimalis (Bloch, 1792)

COMMON NAME: Common Snook

VINCENTIAN NAME: Snook

Figure 10. *Centropomus undecimalis*.

STATUS: Native

RECORDED IN LITERATURE FOR ST. VINCENT: Froese and Pauly (2024).

OCCURRENCE IN THE ST. VINCENT SURVEY: One specimen was captured at station 29, close to the mouth of the Buccament River.

DESCRIPTION: The specimen captured in the survey had a standard length of 363 mm, and weight of 700 g (Figure 10). Maximum reported size 130 cm 23 kg, common to 50 cm 2.2 kg (Orrel, 2003). Body elongated. Prominent dark lateral line which extends to posterior edge of the caudal fin. Snout profile is slightly concave. Lower jaw protrudes beyond the upper. The second dorsal fin has 10 soft rays. The anal fin has 6 soft rays. The row of scales above the lateral line are 67-77 in number. There are 8-10 gill rakers on the lower limb of the first arch (Orrel, 2003).

RANGE: – Florida, south-eastern Gulf of Mexico south to Rio de Janeiro and the Antilles (Orrell, 2003). The range of this species is expanding northwards due to global warming (Purtelbaugh et al., 2020).

HABITAT: – A euryhaline species, able to move between fresh and salt water. Salinity at the point of capture of the specimen in the survey was measured using a refractometer and the water was found to be fresh. Utilises coastal marine, estuarine, hypersaline lagoons and fresh water environments. Found over soft bottoms at less than 50 m depth (Cervigón et al., 1993).

FEEDING AND DIET: Main item in the diet is fish, followed by shrimp.

LIFE CYCLE AND REPRODUCTION: Snook are protandrous hermaphrodites. Males change into females as they increase in size. Males become sexually mature at 1 year and females at 3-4 years. The transition takes place when the fish are between 30 cm and 89 cm in length. Older, larger fish are mostly female.

Spawning takes place in the sea, at river mouths. Larvae are carried by the tide into estuaries and fresh water. Juveniles remain in brackish water until they attain the size of 28cm at which time they utilize coastal marine environments (Staugler, 2019).

CONSERVATION STATUS (IUCN): Least concern

IMPORTANCE TO FISHERIES: Only an opportunistic catch for river fishermen in St. Vincent. Regionally, Common snook are a valued food fish captured by artisanal and sport fishers.

Family: Cichlidae (mouth brooders)

Oreochromis mossambicus (Peters, 1852)

COMMON NAME: Mozambique Tilapia

VINCENTIAN NAMES: Tilapia, Chinee Fish

STATUS: Introduced.

RECORDED IN LITERATURE FOR ST. VINCENT: First record from St. Vincent.

Oreochromis nilocticus, Nile tilapia is reported to have been introduced in 1983 from Dominica as a small-scale aquaculture experiment by the Taiwanese Technical Mission located in the Buccament Valley (Loria, 1993). It is likely that the *O. mossambicus* in the Buccament River originated from the same source.

Figure 11. *Oreochromis mossambicus*, male, captured in the Buccament River.

OCCURRENCE IN THE ST. VINCENT SURVEY: The species was recorded only at station 26, the semi-estuarine pool of the Buccament River (Figure 11). Seven specimens were collected in the survey.

DESCRIPTION: Size of specimens collected in the survey ranged from 46.5 mm – 194 mm standard length. Maximum weight was 300 g.
Dorsal spines 5-18, Dorsal soft rays 11-13, Anal spines 3, Anal soft rays 9-11 (Froese and Pauly, 2024). Gill rakers on first arch 20-22 (FAO Fisheries and Aquaculture Dept., 2024). The characteristics of *O. mossambicus* noted above largely overlap with those of *O. nilocticus*. However, the specimens were identified as *O. mossambicus* due to the absence of narrow dark bars on the caudal fin. In addition, adult males had a distinct duckbill shape of the mouth and red margins on the dorsal and caudal fins.

RANGE: Native range is southeast Africa from Mozambique, south to South Africa (Bills, 2019). Widely introduced in tropical countries world-wide for aquaculture.

HABITAT: In the present survey this species was captured from a semi-estuarine pool with a muddy substrate.
Prefers low flow environments such as ponds, slow flowing rivers, estuaries and creeks. Though largely a freshwater fish it is tolerant of a wide range of salinities and able to survive in low oxygen conditions. A tropical species, which does not tolerate temperatures lower than 15°C (Fofonoff *et al.*, 2018).

FEEDING AND DIET: Omnivorous. Algae mostly diatoms, detritus; larger fish also consume aquatic invertebrates. (Bills, 2019).

LIFE CYCLE AND REPRODUCTION: The life cycle is completed within freshwater. Males dig and defend a crater like "nest" in areas with a sandy or muddy substrate. Females lay eggs in the nest which are fertilized by the male. The female then collects 100-400 eggs in her mouth, where they remain until hatching in 3-5 days. The female broods the hatchlings in the mouth for 10-14 days. Juveniles remain close to the mother and return to her mouth in the event of danger until three weeks old. Capable of rapid reproduction and potential overcrowding (Fofonoff *et al.*, 2018).

CONSERVATION STATUS (IUCN): Vulnerable. Threatened in its native range due to hybridisation with introduced *Oreochromis nilocticus*. Extensive introduction outside its native range for aquaculture. Escapes from fish farms have resulted in *Oreochromis mossambicus* becoming a widespread invasive species with the potential to out-compete native fish for food and nest sites (Fofonoff *et al.*, 2018).

IMPORTANCE TO FISHERIES: Not traditionally targeted by fishermen or widely distributed in the rivers of St. Vincent. Some tilapia (Family Cichlidae) are reared locally in small scale aquaculture ventures by enthusiasts.

Family: Eleotridae (sleepers)

Eleotris perniger (Cope, 1871)

COMMON NAME: Small scaled spinycheek sleeper

VINCENTIAN NAME: Mud Fish, Mud Grouper, Black Gut

Figure 12. *Eleotris perniger*.

STATUS: Native

RECORDED IN LITERATURE FOR ST. VINCENT: Pezold & Cage (2002)

OCCURRENCE IN THE ST. VINCENT SURVEY: Recorded from 11 stations of the St. Vincent survey: 4, 5, 8, 13, 18, 23, 26, 30, 32, 35, 37. Thirty-nine specimens were examined.

DESCRIPTION: Specimens examined in the St. Vincent survey were 21-114 mm in standard length, with a mean standard length of 74.4 mm. Maximum reported standard length is 177 mm (Pezold & Cage, 2002).
A strong forward-facing spine at the lower posterior of the preopercle, embedded in the skin and not clearly visible. Dorsal spines - 7, Dorsal soft rays - 8, Anal spines - 1, Anal soft rays - 8. (Froese and Pauly 2023). Scales in lateral series 54-68, average 60 (Pezold and Gage, 2002). General coloration - dark brown/black. Often exhibits a tan dorsomedial stripe (Figure 12).

RANGE: – Western Atlantic: Florida, Bermuda, the Antilles, the southern Gulf of Mexico, Central America, South America from Colombia to Brazil (Pezold *et al.*, 2019).
There is much confusion in the literature regarding the identification of the various similar species of *eleotrids*. Pezold and Gage (2002) suggest that records of *Eleotris pisonis* from the Antilles likely refer to *Eleotris perniger*.

HABITAT: – In the St. Vincent survey, recorded from 10 semi-estuarine pool stations and 1 foothill torrent station. The highest elevation at which this species was recorded was 45m, restricted to the lower reaches. Found amongst emergent vegetation over a muddy substrate in low flow areas. Common in this habitat.
More often found in freshwater but can tolerate brackish water (Pezold and Gage, 2002). The preferred habitat affinities for this species are benthic, in waters with current velocity 53cm/s and depth 33cm (Coat *et al.*, 2011).

FEEDING AND DIET: Omnivorous. Stomach contents have been found to include plant material, small invertebrates, post larval shrimp and fish (Nordlie, 1981). An ambush predator of the post-larvae and juveniles of diadromous taxa.

LIFE CYCLE AND REPRODUCTION: No gravid females were recorded during the St. Vincent Survey.

Diadromous, possibly amphidromous life cycle. Post larvae have been recorded amongst the tritri (local name for post larval *Sicydium* gobies) run entering freshwater from the sea (Nordlie, 2012). A genetic study confirmed that larvae transitioning from the sea to freshwater were *E. perniger* (Schmidt *et al.*, 2021).

CONSERVATION STATUS (IUCN): Least concern (Pezold *et al.*, 2019).

IMPORTANCE TO FISHERIES: Not targeted by river fishermen.

Gobiomorus dormitor Lacepède, 1800

COMMON NAME: Bigmouth Sleeper

VINCENTIAN NAME: Grouper

STATUS: Native

RECORDED IN THE LITERATURE FOR ST. VINCENT: Froese and Pauly (2023)

OCCURRENCE IN THE SURVEY: Recorded from 8 survey stations; 23, 26, 27, 28, 30, 32, 35, 37. A sample of 13 specimens was examined.

DESCRIPTION: Specimens examined in the St. Vincent survey measured standard length from 34-355 mm, with an average of 168 mm (Figure 13). Maximum reported size is 60 cm total length (Robertson & Van Tassell, 2023).

Dorsal fin spines - 7 (6+1), Dorsal soft rays - 9, Anal fin spines - 1, Anal fin soft rays - 9. Caudal fin rounded with 13-15 rays. Pectoral fins broad. Scales in lateral series 55-64. No lateral line. Body elongated. Mouth large with the lower jaw protruding past the upper jaw. Sexual dimorphism in the urogenital papillae: males pointed, females rounded (Robertson and Van Tassell, 2023).

Figure 13. *Gobiomorus dormitor*.

RANGE: – Southern Florida, Texas south to Brazil, the Antilles (Froese and Pauly, 2023).

HABITAT: – Recorded from 6 semi-estuarine pool and 2 foothill torrent stations in the St. Vincent survey. The highest elevation at which the species was found was 15 m. Benthic. Most common in the lower reaches of the river. Seeks cover under emergent vegetation in semi-estuarine pools and deep pools, boulders and undercut banks in foothill torrents.

A radio telemetry study by Lochmann, Adelsberger & Neal (2015) found that *G. dormitor* in Puerto Rico had a relatively large home range 0.1 -8.1 km, 2.3 km average. Both male and female fish made periodic but uncoordinated migrations into estuarine/marine environments which suggests these movements are not associated with reproduction.

FEEDING AND DIET: Carnivorous. In Costa Rican coastal rivers the diet of *G. dormitor* was largely decapod crustaceans (51%), fish (26%) and aquatic invertebrates (Winemiller and Ponwith, 1981).

LIFE CYCLE AND REPRODUCTION: No reproductive specimens were observed in the St. Vincent survey.

In laboratory experiments, hatching success was greatest in fresh water; 100% mortality occurred within 12 hours post-hatching in salinities of 5 g/l or higher, which suggests that mating and hatching takes place in freshwater (Olivieri-Velázquez and Neal, 2018). In rivers that permit free passage to the sea, juveniles and larvae are reported in brackish water and post larvae enter the river from estuaries and the sea, suggesting larvae develop in salt water (Nordlie, 2012). Self-sustaining populations have, however, been reported where dams block the connection to the sea indicating that the larvae of this species do not always require a saltwater environment to develop. This is supported by a study of chemistry of the core of the otolith formed in the early life stages by Smith and Kwak (2014), which found that 9-12% of *Gobiomorus dormitor* never spent time in saltwater as larvae, showing plasticity in life cycle between individuals. Lochmann (2015) propose that the best description of the life cycle of this species is facultative amphidromous euryhaline.

CONSERVATION STATUS (IUCN): Least Concern (Pezold *et al.*, 2019).

IMPORTANCE TO FISHERIES: One of the fish species most prized by river fishermen in St. Vincent. Fishing methods include shooting with a spear gun, fishing with hook and line, chopping at night with a cutlass, and fishing by hand.

A popular sport fish with anglers in other parts of its range. Research on hatchery rearing of this species has been carried out (Harris *et al.*, 2011), with a view to stocking waters for angling purposes.

Family: Gobiesocidae (Clingfish)

Gobiesox cephalus Lacepède, 1800

A little researched species.

COMMON NAME: Riverine Clingfish

VINCENTIAN NAME: Suckstone

STATUS: Native

RECORDED IN THE LITERATURE FOR ST. VINCENT: Not recorded in the literature for St. Vincent. However, specimens from St. Vincent are lodged in museum collections at the Natural History Museum in London and Royal Ontario Museum (Global Biodiversity Information Facility (GBIF), 2023).

OCCURRENCE IN THE ST. VINCENT SURVEY: Recorded from 6 sample stations in the survey: 8, 9, 27, 33, 35, 37. Six specimens were examined.

DESCRIPTION: Specimens examined in the St. Vincent survey measured 52-133 mm standard length, with an average standard length of 87 mm. Maximum reported size is 15 cm (Robertson & Van Tassell, 2023).

Tear drop shaped (Figure 14i). A single dorsal fin towards rear, with 8-9 soft rays. Anal fin with 7 soft rays. On ventral surface, there is a large sucking disk formed from the pectoral and pelvic fins and a fleshy pad (Figure 14ii). The hexagon shaped structures towards the anterior of the sucking disk are covered with microscopic hair-like structures which conform closely to uneven surfaces and reduce sideways movement, greatly enhancing the efficiency of the sucking disk (Simon 2014). Sensory papillae are located at the front of the sucking disk and in two patches towards the rear. No lateral line. No scales (Robertson & Van Tassell, 2023; Schultz, 1944).

RANGE: – Antilles from Cuba south to Trinidad. In Central America from Honduras to Panama. Northern Colombia and Venezuela. The distribution of this species is based on few records (Ardon & McMahan, 2020).

HABITAT: – Recorded from 3 semi-estuarine pool stations and 3 foothill torrent stations, where the river bottom was a mixture of sand and cobble and strong flow. The highest elevation this species was found in was 34 m and the maximum distance from the sea was 2.6 km.

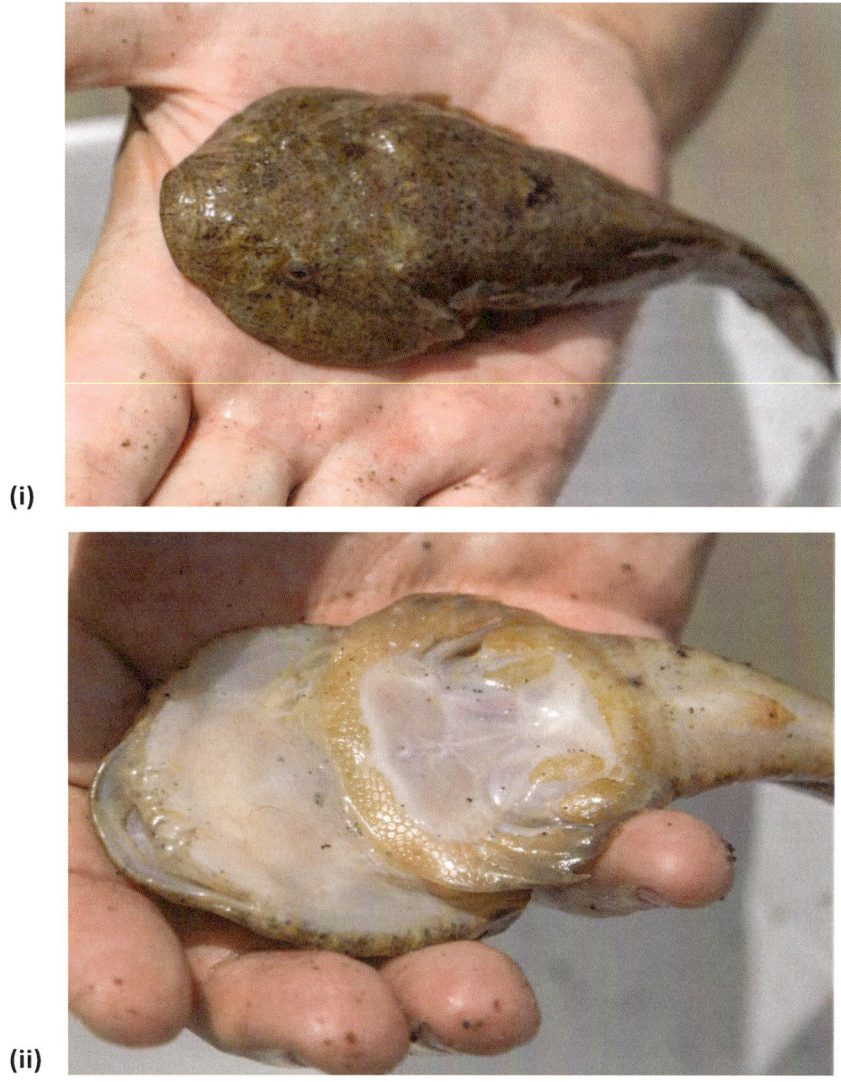

Figure 14. *Gobiesox cephalus* (i) dorsal view (ii) ventral view showing sucking disk.

FEEDING AND DIET: Aquatic insect larvae, mostly Trichoptera (caddis) larvae, make up the majority of the diet. Fish scales are also eaten (Forks *et al.*, 2014).

LIFE CYCLE AND REPRODUCTION: No reproductive specimens found during the St. Vincent survey. A photograph of a sheet of eggs on the surface of a cobble in Rio Chiquito, Costa Rica, posted on GBIF is attributed to this species. Analysis of otolith microchemistry of *G. cephalus* (Frotté *et al.*, 2019) suggests larva development occurs in brackish water; the authors use the term "limited amphidromy" to describe its life cycle.

CONSERVATION STATUS (IUCN): Data Deficient 2020 (Ardon and McMahan, 2020).

River fishermen report that this species is not as frequently observed as in previous years in St. Vincent.

IMPORTANCE TO FISHERIES: Caught incidentally by river fishermen in St. Vincent.

Family: Gobiidae (gobies)

Awaous banana (Valenciennes, 1837)

COMMON NAME: River Goby

VINCENTIAN NAME: Sandfish, Sand Grouper, Bury Sand, Pluffjaw (large adults, Figure 15i)

(i)

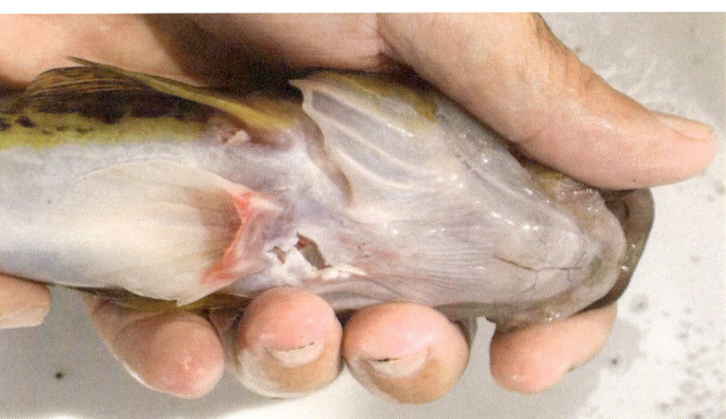

(ii)

Figure 15. *Awaous banana*. (i) *Awaous banana* adult with enlarged cheek. (ii) Ventral view showing fused pelvic fins forming a disk.

STATUS: Native

RECORDED IN THE LITERATURE FROM ST. VINCENT: Watson (1996)

OCCURRENCE IN THE SURVEY: Recorded from 9 stations in the survey: 8, 19, 23, 26, 28, 30, 32,35,37. Nine specimens were examined (Figure 15i).

DESCRIPTION: In the St. Vincent survey the standard lengths observed were 46-225 mm, with an average of 154 mm. Maximum reported standard length: 30 cm - males, 24.4 cm – females (Froese and Pauly, 2023).
Dorsal spines 7-8. Dorsal soft rays 10-12. Anal spine 1. Anal soft rays 9 – 11. The head is broad and blunt. The upper jaw extends beyond the lower jaw, lips large. Pelvic fins fused to form a disk on the ventral surface (Figure 15ii). No lateral line. Body scaled. Scales in lateral series 57-86. (Robertson and Van Tassel, 2023).

RANGE: – Florida, Cuba south to Trinidad. Caribbean coast from Tamaulipas, Mexico south to Caracas, Venezuela (Watson, 1996). Similar species occur on the Pacific side of Central America and the Atlantic coast along South America. Genetic studies have confirmed three separate species (McMahan et al., 2021).

HABITAT: – Recorded from 7 semi-estuarine pools and 2 foothill torrent stations in the St.Vincent survey. Found at elevations from sea level to 29 m.
As the vernacular name suggests, this species is most common over a sandy substrate, occurring in seven survey stations where the substrate was sandy, and the water was clear. It was also recorded from two stations where the substrate was silty, and the water was turbid. These observations concur with Watson (1996). Coat et al. (2011) report that the preferred current velocity is 40cm/s and depth of 39cm.

FEEDING AND DIET: Filamentous algae is the most important item in the diet. Ingests sand and digests the algae and detritus contained in it. Consumes animal prey only when other food is unavailable (Watson, 1996). A study using stable isotope analysis of food sources of freshwater species in Guadeloupe indicates that the diet of A. banana is composed of 60% algae and 33% animal sources (Coat et al., 2009).

LIFE CYCLE AND REPRODUCTION: Facultative amphidromy. Studies of the chemistry of A. banana otoliths (ear bones that grow with the fish and also reflect the growth environment) indicate that adults remain in freshwater. Most larvae develop in a marine environment however 9-12% of otoliths examined show no chemical signature of having lived in saltwater suggesting flexibility in the life cycle (Smith and Kwak, 2014).

CONSERVATION STATUS (IUCN): Least Concern 2019

IMPORTANCE TO FISHERIES: Caught incidentally by river fishermen in St. Vincent using spear guns and hook and line.

Genus: *Sicydium*

INTRODUCTION: *Sicydium* are a genus in the family Gobiidae. There are 16 known species. The majority are found in the Americas; however, 3 species are native to central West Africa. Adult *Sicyduim* inhabit fast flowing streams in tropical and subtropical regions.
The *Sicydium* species of the Antilles have only recently begun to be resolved. Historically, the sporadic nature of collection, the geographical distance between museums where specimens were deposited and the close physical similarity between *Sicydium* species resulted in frequent synonymy

and misidentification. Some clarity was brought by Watson (2000) in which he presented a key to the *Sicydium species* of the Dominican Republic using the morphology of the upper jaw dentition. A genetic study of the *Sicydium* of Puerto Rico by Engman *et al*. (2019) confirmed that the *Sicydium* species described by Watson (2000) were genetically distinct species with the exception of *Sicydium gilberti* which was found to be a hybrid.

Identification of *Sicydium* species using upper jaw dentition requires a microscope and is not possible with live fish in the field. Consequently, in the present survey where *Sicydium* gobies were observed but not sampled they were recorded as *Sicydium* spp.

Sicydium spp.

COMMON NAME: Stone-biting Gobies

VINCENTIAN NAME: Macack (adult), Tritri (post-larvae)

Figure 16. *Sicydium spp.* from the Colonaire River.

STATUS: Native

RECORDED IN THE LITERATURE FOR ST. VINCENT: Recorded as "West Indian Whitebait" by Clark (1905).

OCCURRENCE IN THE SURVEY: Observed from 32 stations: 1, 2, 4, 5, 6, 7, 8, 9, 10, 11, 12, 13, 14, 15, 18, 19, 20, 21, 24, 25, 27, 28, 29, 31, 32, 33, 34, 35, 36, 37, 39, 40.

DESCRIPTION: Small fish, with the largest specimen collected in St. Vincent being 144 mm standard length.

Body robust (Figure 16). Head broad with sensory pores present (Murdy, 2002). Mouth downwardly orientated. Pelvic fins united to form a sucking disk (Figure 17). Two separate dorsal fins. The first dorsal with 6 spines, second dorsal with 1 spine and 9-10 rays. Caudal fin rounded. No lateral line.

Sexual dimorphism is apparent in the shape of the urogenital papilla which is pointed in males (Figure 18a) and rounded with a median depression in females (Figure 18b). The rays of the first dorsal are filamentous in males. Males display bright nuptial colours. General colouration of females is olive brown with dark lateral bands; these are more prominent in younger individuals.

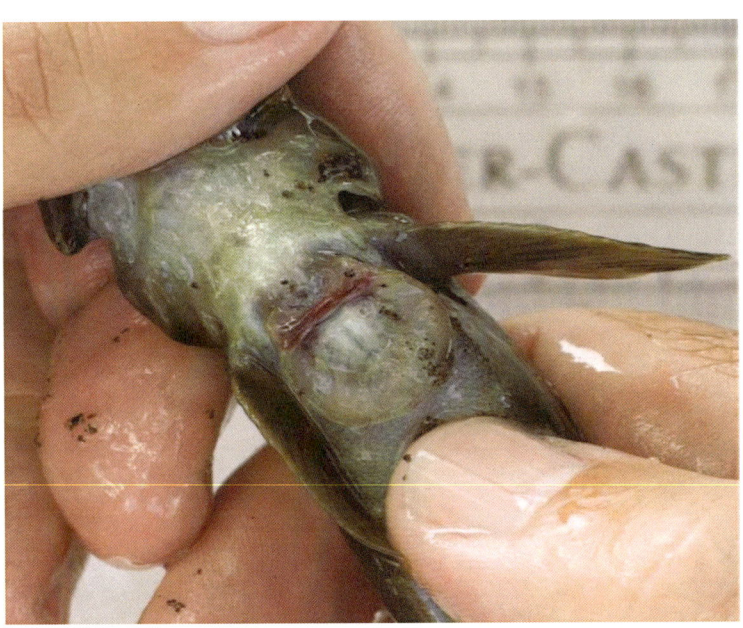

Figure 17. *Sicydium* goby, ventral view showing fused pelvic fins forming a disk.

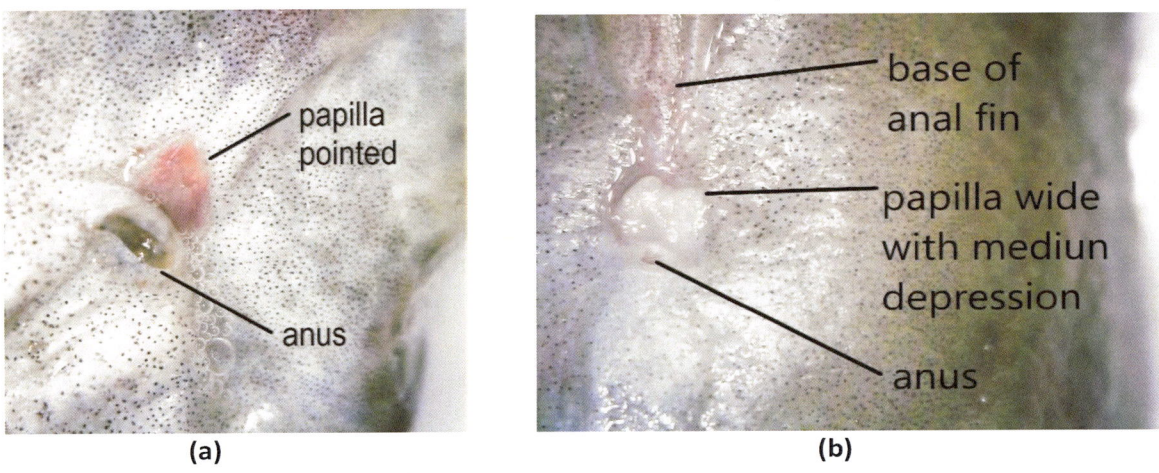

Figure 18. Urogenital Papilla of *Sicydium* gobies (a) male (b) female.

HABITAT: *Sicydium* gobies were the most frequently recorded fish in the St. Vincent survey. Found at 6 semi-estuarine pool stations, 10 foothill torrent stations and 16 mountain torrent stations. They were most abundant in mountain torrent stations. Sicydium were absent from five semi-estuarine pool stations where the substrate is only sand or mud, but present where the substrate is stony.

Occurred from stations near sea level to an altitude of 486 m, the highest station in the St. Vincent survey. The pelvic disk is used to climb waterfalls and to access areas inaccessible to other fish species. *Sicydium* gobies were usually the only fish species recorded from stations above 200 m elevation.

FEEDING AND DIET: Herbivorous. Grazes algal film from the surface of rocks by scraping with the upper teeth (Watson, 2000). The river stones in torrential streams appear clean due to constant grazing by *Sicydium* gobies.

LIFE CYCLE AND REPRODUCTION: Amphidromous. The life cycle of the *Sicydium* gobies was described by Bell (1994) based on research in Dominica (Figure 19).

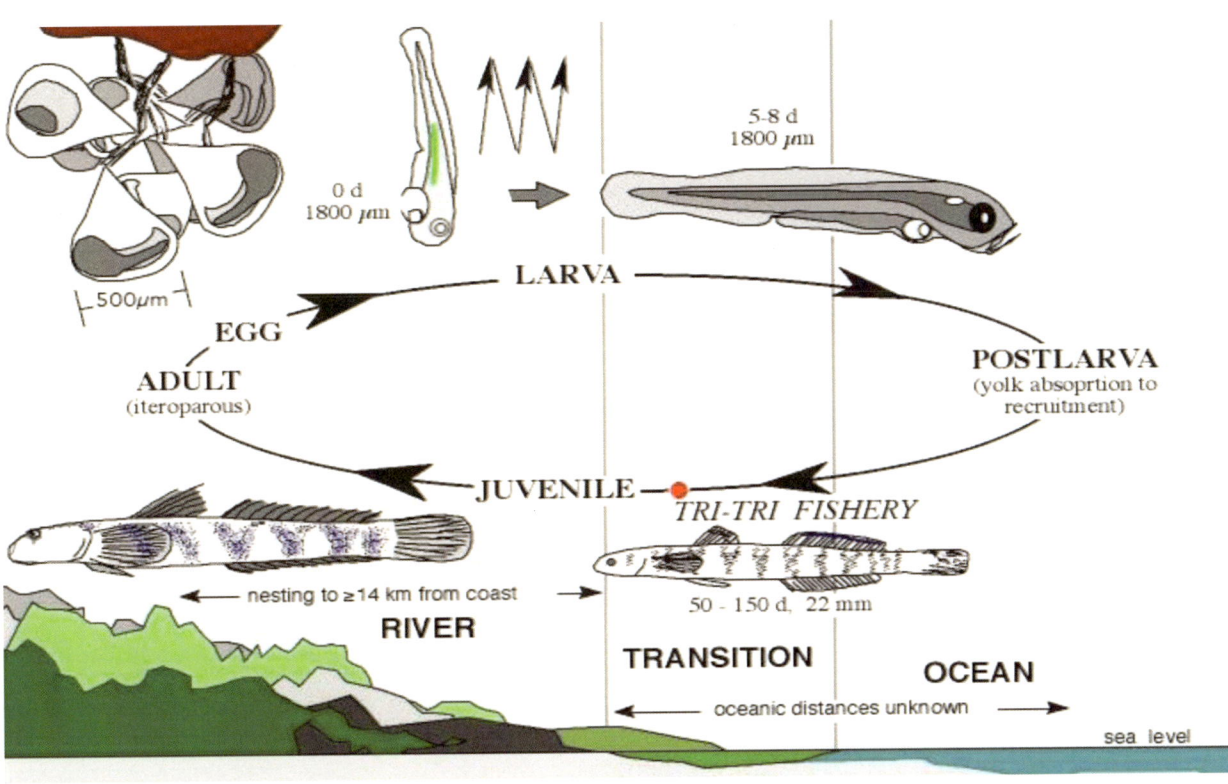

Figure 19. The Lifecycle of Sicydium gobies. (From Bell K.N.I Page on: Gobies Published 2009. http://www.ucs.mun.ca/~kbell/goby/Intro.htm)

Adults reproduce in the river. Males excavate a nest tunnel in gravel at least 10cm deep. The male vigorously defends the territory around the nest from other males, and courts females within it. Mating takes place within the nest. The eggs are laid in clumps attached to each other and to the substrate by microscopic threads. A 45mm female can lay 20,000 – 30,000 eggs in one batch and can spawn again after 14 days (Bell, 2009). The eggs hatch within 1-1.5 days after mating. During the incubation period the male remains in the nest, guards the eggs and cleans them with movements of its fins and body.

On hatching the negatively buoyant larvae repeatedly swim upwards to remain in the current and be transported towards the sea. Larval mortality during this migration is extremely high: Bell (2009) attributes this to predation. The larvae must reach brackish water within 4-5 days in order to survive (Bell and Browne, 1995).

Larvae remain at sea for 50-100 days. When they have attained a length of approximately 22 mm they migrate, en masse, into rivers as post-larvae. Post-larval *Sicydium* are known as tritri in St. Vincent and Martinique, seti in Puerto Rico, ticky-ticky in Jamaica, pisquettes in Guadeloupe, and titiwi in Dominica (Erdman, 1961). The number of individual post-larvae in a single run in a river in Puerto Rico is estimated at 7.3 – 9.4 million (Engman, Kwak and Fischer, 2021). However, the size of the run is variable. Mass migration may be a predator swamping strategy (Bell, 1999) as post-larvae are heavy predated by terns, snooks, grunts, *Gobiomorus* and Eleotrids (Erdman, 1961). Post-larval migration is synchronised by lunar phase and occurs on the 4th day after the last quarter in St. Vincent.

In St. Vincent, the largest post-larval migrations take place between August and December. The months of heaviest rainfall occur between June and November. Freshwater discharge from rivers is less dense than salt oceanic water and remains near the surface for some distance from the river mouth. Post-larvae returning to the river may be guided by salinity gradients that occur in these conditions.

(i)   (ii)

Figure 20. (i) Newly run post-larval *Sicydium*. (ii) Juvenile *Sicydium* after 3 days in fresh water.

When the post-larvae first enter freshwater, they are transparent and pelagic (Figure 20i). Within 3 days the post-larvae develop into benthic juveniles. They become pigmented with dark bands on the body, the mouth orientates downward and scales develop (Figure 20ii). Juveniles disperse into the river system where they later mature into adults. Growth appears to be slow. Bell (2009) reports that a captive female attained a length of only 67 mm standard length at 16.5 years.

IMPORTANCE TO FISHERIES: Macack (Vincentian name for the adults) are targeted by river fishermen in St. Vincent, especially in the Colonaire River. They afford a price of $5.00 XCD per lb. Gear used to catch them include: fishing by hand, spear fishing, cast net, and "sprang" (impounding a section of river). In traditional belief, macack are consumed as an aphrodisiac.

The tritri (post-larvae) fishery is of significant economic and cultural importance in St. Vincent and throughout the Eastern Caribbean. In St. Vincent, tritri is a local delicacy and affords the highest price per pound of any fish or shellfish sold on the local market. A measure, a small rum glass full, sells for $5.00 XCD, a short bucket $200XCD and a long bucket $300.00 XCD (2021 prices).

Fishing has been estimated to capture 5.8-7% of the tritri run in a Puerto Rican study (Engman, Kwak and Fischer, 2021). In St. Vincent, tritri fishing is seasonal with greatest catches occurring between September and January (Figure 21).

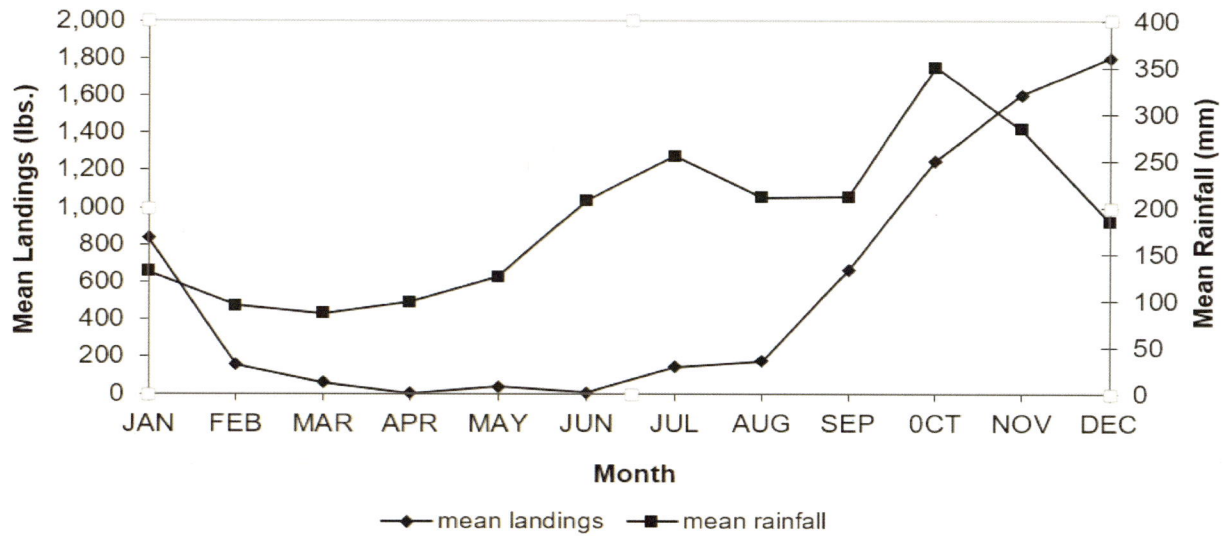

Figure 21. St. Vincent monthly average rainfall and Tritri landings 1998-2007. Data from St. Vincent Fisheries Division.

In St. Vincent, tritri are captured using traditional methods. These include the following.
1. Traps constructed of sacking or agricultural shade net covered in leafy branches and weighed down with river stones. These traps are set in near the river mouth before the run is expected. Migrating tritri seek cover amongst the vegetation in the trap. When the fishers estimate sufficient tritri have entered the trap the corners of the sacking are lifted, the stones removed, and the vegetation beaten to dislodge any tritri attached to it (Figure 22i, ii).

2. Tritri are captured in the sea at the river mouth in the early morning before dawn by attracting migrating post-larvae using light. A flambeau, which is made of a beer bottle or insecticide can filled with kerosene and plugged with a cloth wick attached to the end of a stick, is used as a light source. The flambeau is suspended close to the surface of the sea and held in the corner of a bag made of sacking (Figure 22iii). The bag is lifted when sufficient tritri have entered.

3. A piece of shade net or sacking is used as an improvised seine net which is walked through the migrating tritri and used to scoop them up (Figure 22iv). This method is used in the sea at the river mouth and in the semi-estuarine pools.

Figure 22. Tritri Fishing Methods. (i) Tritri traps in the Richmond River, 2022. (ii) Lifting tritri traps in the Buccament River, 2001. (iii) The flambeau method of tritri fishing. (iv) The seine method of tritri fishing.

The tritri fishery is currently most active in the North Leeward section of the island, with approximately 350 registered fishers in this area, 62% of which are females (Searchlight Newspaper, 2023). The most important fishery takes place in the Wallibou River. Despite the destruction of life in this river by lahars after the 2021 eruption of the La Soufriere volcano, the tritri run still occurred in that year. Tritri fishing is also carried out on the Buccament River and the Colonarie Rivers. Though tritri may run in other rivers consumers resist purchasing from some of these due to concerns regarding water quality. Fishers report that the tritri fishery has declined in recent years. Tritri are highly perishable and must be sold within hours of capture. The higher temperatures experienced as a result of global warming have increased the challenges faced by tritri fishers to market their catch fresh. The UNDP EnGenDER Program 2023 supported tritri fishers through the donation of freezers to strengthen the capacity of female and young tritri fishers to adapt to this impact of climate change.

In addition to its economic value, the tritri fishery has a deeply rooted historical and cultural significance for Vincentians. Price (1966) quotes Brenton (1665) who noted that "Caribs scooped tritri from river mouths" in the French West Indies. The name tritri is thought to be derived from a Carib word (Clark 1910). Traditional tritri fishing techniques, originating from the indigenous people, have been handed down to Vincentians throughout the generations. Tritri are considered a local delicacy and prepared boiled or fried in cakes. These dishes are often the "taste of home" requested by Vincentians living overseas. Tritri has even appeared on postage stamps issued by the Vincentian Government (Figure 23).

Figure 23. Vincentian Postage Stamp, depicting Tritri.

A sample of 77 *Sicydium* gobies were collected during the survey. These were identified to the species level by examination of the upper jaw teeth using a microscope. Three species were found in this sample: *Sicydium plumieri, Sycidium punctatum* and *Sycidium buscki*. These species are discussed separately.

Sicydium plumieri (Bloch, 1786)

COMMON NAME: Plumier's stone-biting Goby, Sirajo

VINCENTIAN NAME: Macack

Figure 24. *Sicydium plumieri*.

STATUS: Native

RECORDED IN THE LITERATURE FOR ST. VINCENT: Froese and Pauly (2023). Specimens were collected from St. Vincent in 1879 and deposited at the National Museum of Natural History, Smithsonian Institution under the synonym *Sicydium vincente* (GBIF, 2023).

OCCURRENCE IN THE SURVEY: Identified at 13 survey stations: 1, 2, 5, 7, 8, 9, 10, 12, 18, 19, 27, 29, 39. *Sicydium plumieri* was found to be the most commonly occurring *Sicydium* species in a sample of 77 *Sicydium* examined. In that sample, 59 specimens (74%) were identified as *S. plumieri* by means of examination of their upper jaw dentition (Figure 24). *Sicydium plumieri* was also found to be the most common *Sicydium* species in Puerto Rico (55%) (Engman *et al.*, 2021).

DESCRIPTION: The largest species of *Sicydium* recorded in the St. Vincent survey. Samples measured were 25.1 -144 mm in standard length, with an average of 84.9 mm. The maximum total length observed in the survey was 173 mm. The maximum size of *S. plumieri* in the St. Vincent survey is similar to that described for the species by Engman *et al.* (2021) for Puerto Rico.

Specimens were identified to the species level, by means of examining the upper jaw dentition which is characterised by two rows of unicuspid teeth (Figure 25) (Watson, 2000).

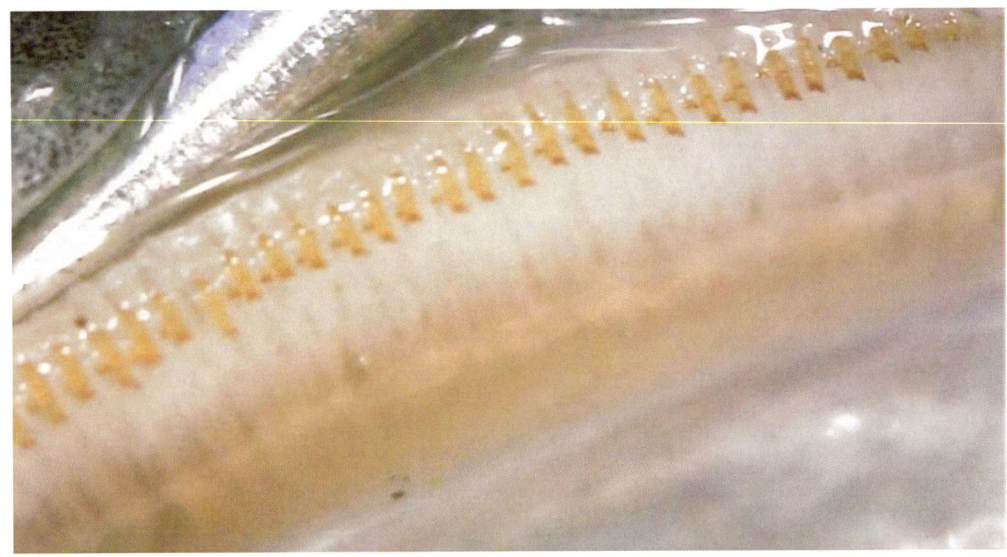

Figure 25. Upper jaw dentition of *Sicydium plumieri*, consisting of two rows of unicuspid teeth.

The general description is as noted in the section on *Sicydium* spp. The mouth is usually larger than in other species of *Sicydium* often extending beyond the posterior margin of the eye. Body colouration is olive brown with darker bands (Figure 24).

Another colour morph was observed (Figure 26) with an orange yellow background with dark brown blotches. This fish is known locally as the "pretty macack". It is a rare form with only 4 specimens captured during the survey ranging in size from 96 -112 mm standard length. Both male and female fish were observed with this colouration. The dentition and comparatively large size suggest *Sicydium plumieri*. However, specimens will be sent to The North Carolina Museum of Natural Sciences for confirmation.

Figure 26. The "Pretty macack". **(Some spear damage is visible near the operculum)**

RANGE: – Antilles to the south of Cuba and Central America (Froese and Pauly, 2023)

HABITAT: – Found at semi-estuarine stations (1), foothill torrent (3) and most commonly at mountain torrent stations (6). Found where the substrate is rocky, and the current is fast flowing.

FEEDING AND DIET: The unicuspid dentition of this species is adapted to scraping algae from the film that covers rocks in the river, hence the name Plumier's stone-biting goby (Watson, 2000). In a study of the stomach contents of *Sicydium* gobies, Monti *et al*. (2018) found that *S. plumieri* favoured species of diatoms more closely attached to the rocks.

LIFE CYCLE AND REPRODUCTION: See *Sicydium* spp. section.

CONSERVATION STATUS (IUCN): Data Deficient (Murdy and Van Tassel, 2010)

IMPORTANCE TO FISHERIES: See *Sicydium* spp. section.

Sicydium punctatum Perugia, 1896

COMMON NAME: Spotted Algae-eating Goby

STATUS: Native

RECORDED IN THE LITERATURE FOR ST. VINCENT: First record from St. Vincent in the literature. A specimen identified as *Sicydium punctatum* was vouchered at the National Museum of Natural History, Smithsonian Institution (GBIF, 2023)

OCCURRENCE IN THE SURVEY: Recorded from 1 location (7 specimens, 10% of *Sicydium* identified to species) in the St. Vincent survey, station 12 on the Colonarie River. A survey in Puerto Rico found 21% of *Sicydium* collected to be *S. punctatum* (Engman *et al*., 2019).

VINCENTIAN NAME: Macack

(i) (ii)

Figure 27. *Sicydium punctatum*. **(i) Specimen identified to species level by dentition (ii) Photograph taken 1st July believed to be a male in nuptial colouration. (Photo S Hornsey)**

DESCRIPTION: Specimens in the St. Vincent survey ranged from 74-90 mm standard length, averaging 72.1 mm standard length (Figure 27). Upper jaw teeth have one row of tricuspid teeth (Figure 28). Males in nuptial colours are a vivid reflective blue with marked V or Y shaped blackish lateral barring (Figure 27ii). The margin of the dorsal is white in large males.

Figure 28. Tricuspid upper jaw teeth of *Sicydium punctatum*.

RANGE: – Antilles from Cuba south to Trinidad. Atlantic Central America from Yucatan south to Venezuela (Pezold, 2015).

HABITAT: – Identified to species level from one location in the St. Vincent survey, station 12 on the Colonarie River. The river at this station is classified as a mountain torrent at an elevation of 207 m, with fast flowing current and a substrate of boulder and cobble. The riparian vegetation is secondary forest. Coat *et al*. (2011) identified the preferred current velocity for the species as 39 cm/s and depth 34 cm. When walking the banks of mountain streams flowing through the forest in early summer when *S. punctatum* is in its blue nuptial colouring these fish can appear abundant. Further sampling of rivers at higher elevations to determine the full distribution of this species is required.

FEEDING AND DIET: Watson (2000) states that the less robust tricuspid teeth of *S. punctatum* are adapted for consumption of filamentous algae and softer vegetation, hence the name algae-eating goby. A study of the stomach contents of *Sicydium* gobies by Monti *et al.* (2018) found that *S. punctatum* favoured pedunculate diatoms which are less firmly attached to the substrate. A tank study by Barbegron *et al.* (2017) in which captive fish were observed grazing on cobbles brought from the river found that *S. punctatum* fed by scraping diatoms and blue green algae from the surface of rocks but filamentous algae were not consumed. In this study, dominant males heavily grazed on preferred rocks only, although other fish also grazed there (Barbegron *et al.*, 2017). This behaviour was found to promote the growth of preferred diatom species and is known as "gardening".

LIFE CYCLE AND REPRODUCTION: See *Sicydium* spp. section.

CONSERVATION STATUS (IUCN): Least concern 2011. Population trend decreasing (Pezold, 2015).

IMPORTANCE TO FISHERIES: See *Sicydium* spp. section.

Sicydium buscki Evermann & Clark, 1906

COMMON NAME: Busck's stone-biting Goby

VINCENTIAN NAME: Macack

STATUS: Native

RECORDED IN THE LITERATURE FOR ST. VINCENT: First record from St. Vincent.

OCCURRENCE IN THE SURVEY: Recorded from 4 stations in the St. Vincent survey: 8, 9, 12, 19. Eleven of the 77 (16%) *Sicydium* identified to species were found to be *Sicydium buscki*.

Figure 29. *Sicydium buscki*, unicuspid upper jaw dentition.

RANGE: - Cuba, Dominican Republic and Puerto Rico (Watson, 2000). Museum specimens identified as *S. buscki*, collected in Dominica, are vouchered in the collection of fishes at Texas A&M University (GBIF, 2023).

HABITAT: – Recorded from semi-estuarine pool (1), foothill torrent (2) and mountain torrent (1) stations at elevations from near sea level to 207 m. Found in fast flowing water over stony substrates

FEEDING AND DIET: The unicuspid dentition of this species is adapted to scraping algae from the film that covers rocks in the river, hence the name Busck's stone-biting goby (Watson, 2000).

LIFE CYCLE AND REPRODUCTION: See *Sicydium* spp. section.

CONSERVATION STATUS (IUCN): Data deficient.

IMPORTANCE TO FISHERIES: See *Sicydium* spp. section.

Family: Haemulidae (grunts)

Rhonciscus crocro (Cuvier, 1830)

COMMON NAME: Burro grunt

VINCENTIAN NAME: Crocro (named for the croaking nose made, using the pharyngeal teeth, on capture)

STATUS: Native

RECORDED IN LITERATURE FOR ST. VINCENT: Froese and Pauly (2023)

OCCURRENCE IN THE ST. VINCENT SURVEY: Observed at 11 stations in the survey: 4, 10, 18, 23, 26, 28, 32, 33, 35, 37, 39. Fifteen specimens were examined.

DESCRIPTION: Standard length of specimens in the St. Vincent survey ranged from 16.4-278 mm, with an average standard length of 115.4 mm. The maximum reported size for this species is 38 cm total length, and weight of 1.9 kg (Froese & Pauly, 2023).
Body elongate, deep and compressed (Figure 30). Dorsal fin with 13 spines and 11-13 rays. Anal fin with 3 spines and 6-7 rays, with the second spine being longest. Anal fin scaled at base (Snow, 2023).

RANGE: – Florida, the Antilles, Matagorda Bay Texas south to Brazil (Lindeman *et al.*, 2019).

Figure 30. *Rhonciscus crocro*, captured from the Wallibou River, March 2023.

HABITAT: —Recorded from stations classified as semi-estuarine pools (7) and foothill torrents (3) in the present survey. Never found more than 1 km from the sea; maximum elevation 80 m. Recorded from the lower reaches of the Wallibou River (station 40) 24 months after pyroclastic flows and lahars resulting from the 2021 eruption of La Soufriere which completely destroyed life in that river. These fish must therefore have recolonised from the sea.
Found in brackish water, estuaries, bays and freshwater. The species is known to ascend the Usumacina River, Mexico a distance of 370 km from the sea (Hernandez-Gomez *et al.*, 2021). Demersal. Maximum depth 15 m. Found in fast and slow current (Froese and Pauly, 2023).

FEEDING AND DIET: Crustaceans and small fish (Snow, 2023).

LIFE CYCLE AND REPRODUCTION: Diadromous. Little is known regarding reproduction. Land locked populations are known from Veracruz, Mexico, suggesting that a marine environment is not obligatory for completion of the life cycle (Snow, 2023).

CONSERVATION STATUS (IUCN): Data Deficient (Lindeman *et al.*, 2019).

IMPORTANCE TO FISHERIES: Targeted by river fishermen in St. Vincent, most frequently using spear guns and hook and line gear. Regionally, also caught by artisanal fishermen using beach seine nets (Snow, 2023).

Family: Lutjanidae (snappers)

Lutjanus jocu (Bloch and Schneider, 1801)

COMMON NAME: Dog snapper

VINCENTIAN NAME: River snapper

Figure 31. *Lutjanus jocu*.

STATUS: Native

RECORDED IN LITERATURE FOR ST. VINCENT: Froese and Pauly (2023).

OCCURRENCE IN THE ST. VINCENT SURVEY: Recorded from 2 stations (18, 32) during the survey.

DESCRIPTION: One juvenile of 76.1 mm standard length recorded in the St. Vincent survey (Figure 31). Maximum size 128 cm, 28.6 kg (Froese and Pauly, 2023).
Deep bodied. Canines in upper jaw large. Dorsal fin continuous with 10 spines and 13-14 soft rays. The base of the dorsal and anal fins scaled. Scales in lateral series 46-49. A blue line below the eye and across the operculum continuous in juveniles, broken in adults (Figure 31). A pale triangle sometimes visible below eye (Anderson, 2003).

RANGE: – Massachusetts south to northern Brazil, the Antilles (Anderson, 2003).

HABITAT: – Recorded from semi-estuarine pool stations.

Adults inhabit coral reefs, juveniles (< 7 cm T.L.) frequent estuarine environments (Moura *et al.*, 2011). Juveniles occasionally enter rivers (Anderson, 2003).

FEEDING AND DIET: Diet includes fish, crustaceans, gastropods and cephalopods (Anderson, 2003).

LIFE CYCLE AND REPRODUCTION: Spawning aggregations occur in the marine environment. One is known to take place in the sea off Belize in January; otherwise, solitary with a home range (Anderson, 2003).

CONSERVATION STATUS (IUCN): Data deficient (Lindeman *et al.*, 2019).

IMPORTANCE TO FISHERIES: Not targeted by river fishermen in St. Vincent.
Exploited regionally by artisanal and industrial marine capture fisheries using hand lines, fish pots and gill nets.

Family: Megalopidae (tarpons)

Megalops atlanticus (Valenciennes, 1847)

COMMON NAME: Tarpon

VINCENTIAN NAME: Bass

Figure 32. Juvenile *Megalops atlanticus* captured from the semi-estuarine pool of the Buccament River.

STATUS: Native

RECORDED IN LITERATURE FOR ST. VINCENT: Froese and Pauly (2023)

OCCURRENCE IN THE ST. VINCENT SURVEY: 1 specimen captured from station 26 in the St. Vincent survey.

DESCRIPTION: The fish recorded in the survey was 355 mm standard length (Figure 32). A tarpon of this length is a juvenile approximately 1 year old (Crabtree, Cyr and Dean, 1995). Maximum reported total length 250 cm, maximum weight 161 kg (Froese and Pauly, 2023).
Mouth large, orientated upwards, lower jaw extends beyond upper (Figure 32). Dorsal fin short with 12-15 rays; the final ray forms a long filament. Pelvic and pectoral fins low on the body. Scales large and stiff. Lateral line present. Bright silver in colour.

RANGE: – Western Atlantic: Virginia, Bermuda south to central Brazil. The Antilles. Eastern Atlantic: Mauritania south to Angola. Eastern Pacific: Traversed the Panama Canal to the Pacific coast of Panama (Froese and Pauly, 2023).

HABITAT: Recorded from one semi-estuarine pool station in the St. Vincent Survey.
Utilises a wide range of habitats including freshwater rivers and lakes, estuaries, mangroves, coastal waters, bays and hypersaline lagoons. Tolerates salinities from $0 - 45\ °/_{oo}$. The swim bladder is adapted to function as a gas exchange surface allowing tarpon to survive in poorly oxygenated waters by gulping air from the surface. Typically found at depths of 0-15 m (Adams et al., 2019).

FEEDING AND DIET: Young juveniles feed on zooplankton, small crustaceans and insects. Older juveniles and adults utilise a greater range of prey including shrimp, swimming crabs, polychaete worms and fish. (Adams et al., 2019).
The head and mouth parts of tarpon are adapted for suction feeding – rapid expansion of the cranium and opening of the jaw draws water and prey into the mouth. Tarpon can ingest small prey fish within 20 milliseconds in this manner (Gidmark et al., 2019).

LIFE CYCLE AND REPRODUCTION: Adults aggregate in coastal waters before migrating offshore to spawn. The eggs hatch into planktonic larvae called leptocephali (phase 1). Leptocephalus are eel like in shape, transparent and 26 mm in length. After 20-40 days the larvae are carried by currents and tides to sheltered inshore habitats. A metamorphosis then takes place marked by a reduction in size to 14 mm (phase II). Phase II is followed by growth to approximately 40 mm and the development of scales (phase III). Phase II, III and juvenile tarpon are found in salt marsh, mangroves, stagnant pools with low oxygen environments where they are protected from predation. Tarpon are a long lived fish and are known to live for 50 years in the wild and reach sexual maturity at 7-10 years at 80-120 cm in length (Adams et al., 2019).

CONSERVATION STATUS (IUCN): Vulnerable due to an estimated regional population decline of 30%. Threats to the species include commercial harvesting outside of the USA, effects of recreational fishing, including catch and release fishing, habitat loss, habitat fragmentation, habitat degradation and decline in water quality (Adams et al., 2019).

IMPORTANCE TO FISHERIES: Not targeted by river fishermen in St. Vincent. Regionally important artisanal and sport marine capture fisheries. Prized by sport fishers due to its large size and fighting ability.

Family: Mugilidae (mullets)

Dajaus monticola (Bancroft, 1834)

COMMON NAME: Mountain mullet

VINCENTIAN NAME: Mountain mullet

Figure 33. *Dajaus monticola*.

STATUS: Native

RECORDED IN LITERATURE FOR ST. VINCENT: St. Vincent and the Grenadines Fifth National Report to The United Nations Convention on Biodiversity (2015).

OCCURRENCE IN THE ST. VINCENT SURVEY: Recorded from 24 stations in the survey; 4, 5, 6, 8, 9, 10, 11, 12, 13, 14, 15, 18, 19, 23, 24, 26, 30, 32, 33, 35, 36, 37, 39, 40 (Figure 33). 152 specimens were examined. Widely and frequently recorded in the survey: (i) equal in occurrence at stations with *Eleotris perniger* in semi-estuarine pools and (ii) second in frequency to *Sycydium* spp. in foot hill and mountain torrent stations.

DESCRIPTION: Specimens in the St. Vincent survey measured 29-198 mm in standard length, with an average standard length of 80.6 mm. Maximum recorded size is 36 cm total length (Froese and Pauly, 2023).
Head convex between the eyes, no transparent eyelid. Dorsal spines 5, dorsal soft rays 8. Anal spines 2, anal soft rays 9. 40 (38-35) scales in lateral series. No lateral line. Dark scale edges form a criss-cross pattern on the body (Robertson and Van Tassel, 2023) (Figure 33).

RANGE: In the Western Atlantic from North Carolina, Gulf of Mexico south to Venezuela and the Antilles. In the Eastern Pacific, from Southern California to Ecuador (GBIF, 2023).

HABITAT: – Recorded from semi-estuarine pools (10), foothill torrents (7), and mountain torrents (7). Found at stations with elevations from sea level to 217 m in the St. Vincent survey.
Found with *Rhonciscus crocro* from the lower reaches of the Wallibou River (station 40) 24 months after pyroclastic flows and lahars resulting from the 2021 eruption of La Soufriere which completely

destroyed life in that river. *Dajanus monticola* were relatively abundant at this station, 19 samples were collected, ranging from 66 to 115 mm in standard length.

Dajaus monticola is found in freshwater, brackish and marine environments. A pelagic species. Frequents rivers with strong current, stony substrate and clear water (Cruiz, 1987). Ascends streams to the upper reaches, when unimpeded by barriers, and has been recorded at elevations of 1500m (Snow, 2023). Adults are often solitary. Juveniles are found in schools at river mouths in brackish water.

FEEDING AND DIET: Omniverous. In Jamaica, wide range of aquatic insects predominate the diet, followed by algae and shrimp (Aiken, 1998). Phillip (1993) recorded insects, prawns, fruits and algae from the stomachs of *D. monticola* from Trinidad.

LIFE CYCLE AND REPRODUCTION: Two gravid females, 198 mm and 122 mm standard length were recorded from the semi-estuarine pool of the Petit Bordel River (station 35) in April 2023. Diadromous. Larvae have been recorded from the sea, and juveniles in rivers. It is unclear if reproduction occurs in fresh water with the eggs being carried out to the sea by the current of the river (amphidromy), or if adults migrate to the sea reproduce, and then return to fresh water (catadromy) (NatureServe & Lyons, 2019). The spawning season varies across the region (Aiken, 1998). Males reach sexual maturity at 9.6 cm and females at 12.3 cm (Froese and Pauly, 2024).

CONSERVATION STATUS (IUCN): Least concern. The population is stable. This species is common and widely distributed (NatureServe & Lyons, 2019).

IMPORTANCE TO FISHERIES: Frequently targeted by river fishermen in St. Vincent. The most common gear used is hook and line (Figure 34). Bait used includes bread and banana when the water is clear and worms when the water is coloured due to rain. Other methods and gear used are hand and spear fishing. *Dajaus monticola* support important fisheries regionally, especially in Mexico (Snow, 2023).

Figure 34. Hook and line fishing for *Dajaus monticola* in the Yambou River.

Mugil curema Valenciennes, 1836

COMMON NAME: White mullet

VINCENTIAN NAME: Bosun, Shit Bosun

Figure 35. *Mugil curema*.

STATUS: Native

RECORDED IN LITERATURE FOR ST. VINCENT: Froese and Pauly (2023)

OCCURRENCE IN THE ST. VINCENT SURVEY: Recorded from 5 stations in the St. Vincent survey: 8, 23, 26, 32, 37. Eight specimens were examined.

DESCRIPTION: Sizes ranged from 58 to 420 mm standard length in the St. Vincent survey. Maximum size 91 cm, common to 35 cm (Harrison, 2002).
Dorsal surface of head flattened. Body elongated. Adipose eyelid present. Three spines and 9 soft rays in the anal fin. Origin of 1st dorsal fin equidistant between tip of the snout and the base of the tail. 36-39 scales in longitudinal series. Second dorsal and anal fin well scaled (Harrison, 2002). Body silvery (Figure 35). A dark mark at the base of the pectoral fin and a gold patch on the upper opercle.

RANGE: Western Atlantic: Cape Cod to Southern Brazil, Bermuda, Gulf of Mexico, the Caribbean. Eastern Atlantic: Cape Verde Islands, Senegal to Namibia. Eastern Pacific: Gulf of California to Chile (Froese and Pauly, 2023).

HABITAT: – Reported from coastal marine areas, hypersaline lagoons and estuaries and occasionally freshwater. Juveniles are found in estuaries and mangroves and have been reported from freshwater as far as 700 km from the river mouth in the Lacantún River, Mexico (Rodiles-Hernandez *et al.*, 2005). The ratio of barium and calcium deposited in layers on the otoliths (ear bones) is indicative of the environment of the fish over time. A study of this type in Mexico identified a variety of different habitat use strategies by white mullet: 27% remained in high salinity environments, 30% made sporadic use of estuaries, 13% used freshwater for short periods and 30% used estuarine frequently and occasionally entered freshwater (Mia *et al.*, 2018). Occurs over sandy and muddy substrates in clear and turbid water to depths of 0-25 m. A schooling species.

This species was confined to semi-estuarine pool habitat in the present survey. Larger mullet were observed to retreat to the sea when disturbed.

FEEDING AND DIET: The diet of juveniles is composed of plankton. Adults consume detritus and fine particulate matter (Carpenter, 2002). The diet of *Mugil curema* in a coastal lagoon in Mexico was found to be 97% composed of diatoms, a type of unicellular alga (Rudea, 2002). Diatoms adhere to the surface of sand, mud and detritus particles, which are ingested by the mullet. An elongated gut assists in processing this food.

LIFE CYCLE AND REPRODUCTION: Adults are believed to migrate in schools offshore to spawn. On hatching the larvae migrate to estuarine habitats until reaching sexual maturity which is attained at 18-21 cm in length and 2-3 years of age. Spawning seasons vary over the range of the species (Castro *et al.*, 2019).

CONSERVATION STATUS (IUCN): Least concern. A widely distributed and common species.

IMPORTANCE TO FISHERIES: Opportunistically caught by river fishermen in St. Vincent.

Supports important commercial gill net and trap fisheries in the USA, Mexico, Venezuela and Brazil (Castro *et al.*, 2019).

Family: Poeciliidae (livebearers)

Poecilia reticulata Peters, 1859

COMMON NAME: Guppy

VINCENTIAN NAME: Million fish, Millions

Figure 36. A wild-caught male *Poecilia reticulata*.

STATUS: Introduced into the Caribbean outside its native range, Trinidad, Venezuela, and Guyana, within the last 150 years (Deacon, 2023).

RECORDED IN LITERATURE FOR ST. VINCENT: No record exists in the literature for this species for St. Vincent. However, specimens identified as *Poecilia reticulata* were collected here and are lodged at the Natural History Museum, London. (GBIF, 2023)

OCCURRENCE IN THE ST. VINCENT SURVEY: Recorded from 2 sample stations (20 and 21) in the present survey.

DESCRIPTION: A small species. Four specimens examined in the St. Vincent survey ranged from 14.9 to 18.7 mm standard length, with an average standard length of 17.2 mm.
Exhibits sexual dimorphism. 1 Dorsal fin with no spines, 7-8 rays. Origin of dorsal behind the origin of the origin of the anal fin in females) and below in males. Anal fin in males modified to form an elongated reproductive organ (gonopodium). 25-28 scales in lateral series. In females the anal fin is rounded (Carpenter, 2012).
Males are smaller (15-20 mm standard length) than females (20-25 mm standard length) in natural conditions (Deacon, 2023). Colouration in males is conspicuous and varied including orange, green and black spots (Figure 36). A black spot is often located at the base of the tail. Females are silver in colour. The body is deeper than that of the male.
Guppies are a popular species amongst aquarists and many ornamental varieties have been bred. Ornamental varieties are larger than wild fish, reaching 35 mm in males and 60 mm in females. Male ornamentals have large and colourful dorsal and caudal fins.

RANGE: – This species is native to Northeastern South America and Trinidad and Tobago. Widely introduced for mosquito control and human release of unwanted pets. Now occurs in more than 70 countries outside of its native range. Found in tropical and subtropical regions on all continents, with the exception of Antarctica (Deacon & Magurran, 2016).

HABITAT: – In the present study, the only location where this species was found was a headwater stream near the Montreal water catchment (station 21), at an elevation of 485 m. The water was clear, flow was low and depth averaged 25 mm. *Poecilia reticulata* is not common in rivers in St. Vincent but is known to occur in freshwater habitats not included in the survey e.g., drains in Paul's Lot an urban area in Kingstown, a clear spring flowing through *Commelina diffusa* (water grass) in Penniston.
Inhabits a wide range of habitats including clear, vegetated springs and mountain streams at higher altitudes, drainage ditches and ponds. Survives in brackish and hypersaline water. Favours low flow, vegetated, shallow habitats with reduced predation pressure (Froese and Pauly, 2023). Tolerant of water pollution and anthropogenic disturbance (Gomes-Silva *et al.*, 2020).

FEEDING AND DIET: Benthic algae and aquatic insect larvae (Dussault and Kramer, 1981).

LIFE CYCLE AND REPRODUCTION: A gravid female 18.7 mm standard length was collected on 13th March during the St. Vincent survey.
Completes its life cycle within freshwater. Courtship involves a sequential series of body posturing, followed by internal fertilisation where sperm are introduced into the female via the male's gonopodium. Females are polygamous and may be fertilized by several males. Sperm can remain viable in the female's body for up to 8 months. This species is ovoviviparous – the fertilized eggs develop within the female, nourished by the yolk sack, until the time of hatching. The gestation period is 4-6 weeks, and the maximum brood size is 100 young. Juveniles are able to feed immediately upon hatching and there is no parental care. *P. reticulata* is highly prolific. Females become sexually mature in 78-91 days. The inter-brood period is 25-31 days (Deacon, 2023; Lyons, 2021).

CONSERVATION STATUS (IUCN): Least concern (Lyons, 2023). Widely introduced for the purpose of mosquito control. Has potential to negatively impact native species by the introduction of parasites, competition and predation (Deacon, 2023).

IMPORTANCE TO FISHERIES: Not targeted by river fishermen. Sometimes captured in the wild in St. Vincent for release into aquaria and ponds for ornamental purposes or barrels for collection of rainwater to control mosquitos.
Internationally this species is often used as a subject for scientific research in genetic and behavioural studies because it is small, robust, easy to maintain in captivity and reproduces prolifically.

Family: Syngnathidae (pipefish)

Microphis lineatus (Kaup, 1856)

NOTE ON CLASSIFICATION: This species was formerly known as *Microphis brachyurus*. Four subspecies were recognised: *Microphis brachyurus brachyurus* from the Central Indian Ocean, *Microphis brachyurus millepunctatus* from the Western Indian Ocean, *Microphis brachyurus aculeatus* from the Eastern Central Atlantic and *Microphis brachyurus lineatus* from the Western Central Atlantic (Dawson, 1984). In recent publications, the former subspecies are now classified as four distinct species. The species found in the Western Central Atlantic is now *Microphis lineatus* (Froese and Pauly, 2023).

COMMON NAME: Opossum pipefish

VINCENTIAN NAME: Tritri Pirate

STATUS: Native

RECORDED IN LITERATURE FOR ST. VINCENT: Froese and Pauly (2023).

OCCURRENCE IN THE ST. VINCENT SURVEY: Recorded from 4 stations in the survey: 26, 30, 32, 35. Twenty-seven specimens were examined.

DESCRIPTION: In the St. Vincent survey, specimens ranged in size from 81 to 189 mm total length, averaging 148 mm in total length. Maximum size 194 mm standard length (Gilmore, 2009). Extremely elongated. Body encased in jointed bony rings, 16-21 on the trunk and 20-26 on the tail. Fins are small, making them poor swimmers: 37-50 rays on dorsal fin, 17-23 rays on pectoral fin, 9 rays on caudal fin. Mouth is small and sits at the end of a tubular snout (Figure 37i).
Body of adults is yellow brown colour. Males in reproductive condition have red patches on each trunk ring and strong red markings on the lower snout.

(i)

(ii)

Figure 37. *Microphis lineatus*. (i) Specimens showing head. (ii) A ventral view of a section of the brood pouch of a male containing eggs. (The specimen was 186mm TL and captured at the mouth of the Petite Bordel River on 17 April, 2023. The embryos were well developed and were in the pre-hatch stage.)

RANGE: – Non-breeding records from the Carolinas and northern Gulf of Mexico. Breeding populations from eastern Florida, the Antilles, Mexico, Atlantic Central America south to Brazil (Froese and Pauly, 2023). Reported to have entered Eastern Pacific via the Panama Canal (GBIF, 2023).

HABITAT: – In the present study, this species was recorded only from semi-estuarine pools on the leeward side of the island. These locations are characterised by low flow and a muddy substrate. Specimens were always captured from amongst emergent vegetation.

Adults are found in freshwater and low salinity habitats and are associated with emergent vegetation (Frias-Torres, 2002).

FEEDING AND DIET: Feed on insect larvae, juvenile fish and small crustaceans. Ambush predators that often hanging vertically to mimic a plant stem when waiting for prey. Feed during the day (Frias-Torres, 2002).

LIFE CYCLE AND REPRODUCTION: Reproduction takes place in fresh water. Like their relatives the seahorses, it is the male pipefish who broods the eggs. On mating the female deposits an average of around 400 eggs into a pouch under the body of the male (Figure 37ii). The eggs remain in the brood pouch until hatching 5-10 days later. Reproduction takes place in the wet season in Florida (Gilmore, 2009) and year-round in Mexico (Miranda-Marure and Martínez-Pérez, 2004). Males can brood sequential batches of eggs.

There is no further parental care after the eggs hatch. The larvae require brackish/marine water conditions to survive and are carried to the river mouth by the current. The pelagic larvae develop in the sea and juveniles of 70 mm are known to associate with floating *Sargassum*. Once the juveniles have grown sufficiently, they migrate into freshwater. Sexual maturity is attained at 90 mm in males and 110 mm in females (Miranda-Marure and Martínez-Pérez, 2004).

Reproductive fish were observed in the St. Vincent survey. One gravid female, 179 mm total length, released eggs on capture on 6 March 2023. Brooding males were also observed, 4 of 14 males (29%), 158-176 mm total length, were observed on 17 April 2023 with eggs in the brood pouch (Figure 37ii). Reproductive specimens were recorded at the height of the dry season in St. Vincent. Further study is required to confirm year-round breeding in St. Vincent.

CONSERVATION STATUS (IUCN): Data Deficient (NatureServe, Sparks & Lyons, 2019).

NOAA (National Marine Fisheries Service) has listed *M. lineatus* as a species of concern in Florida due to a decreasing population (Gilmore, 2009). Habitat destruction, waterway engineering, declining water quality, disease and removal of freshwater vegetation are identified as causative factors. Similar activities taking place in St. Vincent would therefore threaten this species.

IMPORTANCE TO FISHERIES: Not targeted by river fishermen in St. Vincent.

Freshwater and Brackish Water Decapod Crustaceans

Infraorder Caridea – True Shrimp

The species fresh and brackish water shrimp recorded in the St. Vincent Survey are summarised in Table 5.

Table 5. An inventory of shrimp species identified during the survey.

Scientific Name	Vernacular Names	Common Name	St. Vincent Stations Where Species was Recorded	Total Number of Stations Where Species Occurred
Family Atyidae				
Atya innocous	Bookie	Basket Shrimp	1,2,6,7,12,15,16,18, 20,21,24,25,31,34,38	15
Atya scabra	Bookie, Army Bookie	Camacuto Shrimp	14	1
Jonga serri	None	Crevette	17,26,28,32,35	5
Micratya poeyi	None	Dwarf Caribbean Filter Shrimp	1,2,6,16,20,21,31,34	8
Family Xiphocarididae				
Xiphocaris elongata	Lobster Leader, Jumper	Yellow-Nosed Shrimp, Salpiche, Piquine	6,25,26,31,36	5
Family Palaemonidae Subfamily Palaeoninae				
Macrobrachium acanthurus	Yambou, Swampy Salt Pond Crayfish	Cinnamon River Shrimp	23,26,32,35,37	5
Macrobrachium carcinus	River Lobster	Big Claw River Shrimp	2,5,7,14,15,26,27,28, 29,38	10
Macrobrachium crenulatum	Glass Bottle, Bottleman, Yellow Tail, Madras, Blue Bean, Blue Man	Camarón Bocú	6,7,9,10,11,19,20,23, 25,31,32,34	12
Macrobrachium faustinum	Grass Tail, Bus Finger	Caribbean Long Arm Shrimp	9,11,13,14,17,19,23, 26,27,29,33,36,37	13
Macrobrachium heterochirus	Colonarie, Bamboo, Antigua, Malatar	Cascade River Prawn	2,6,8,9,10,12,18,20, 21,24,25,27,29,31, 34,37	16

The majority of freshwater shrimp, known locally as "crayfish", found in in St. Vincent belong to three Families.
1. The Family Atyidae. Shrimps in this family can be recognised by the fingers of the first and second pereiopods (walking legs) ending in brush like bristles.
2. The Family Xiphocarididae formerly classified in the Atyidae. Fingers of the first and second periopods do not end in brush-like structures but delicate pincers.
3. The Family Palaemonidae, Genus *Macrobrachium*. In these species the first and second legs end in well-developed pincers known locally as "gundies".

Family: ATYIDAE

Atya innocous (Herbst, 1792)

COMMON NAME: Basket shrimp, Camacuto shrimp

VINCENTIAN NAME: Bookie

Figure 38. *Atya innocous*.

Figure 39. Illustration of *Atya innocous* male. (Artist Madeleine Smith)

STATUS: Native

RECORDED IN LITERATURE FOR ST. VINCENT: Chance and Hobbs (1969), Harrison and Rankin (1976).

OCCURRENCE IN THE ST. VINCENT SURVEY: Recorded from 15 survey stations; 1, 2, 6, 7, 12, 15, 16, 18, 20, 21, 24, 25, 31, 34, 38. A sample of 170 specimens was examined.

DESCRIPTION: Chelea of the first and second periopods end in brush-like structures. Walking legs are robust: an ambulatory species. The largest Atyid shrimp species in the survey: carapace lengths (CL) from 3.8 to 37.0 mm were observed, with an average CL of 15.4 mm. The maximum reported total length is 12.2 cm (Fryer, 1977a). Males are larger and more robust than females. The colour varies from mottled brown to dark olive green, almost black in large specimens (Figures 38 and 39). Some individuals have a tan dorsomedial stripe.

RANGE: – Central America - the Pacific and Atlantic slopes of Nicaragua, Costa Rica and Panama. The Antilles from Cuba south to Trinidad (Hobbs and Hart, 1982).

HABITAT: – Reported from semi-estuarine pool (1 station), foot hill torrent (1 station) and headwater streams (1) but was most frequently found at mountain torrent stations (12 stations). Recorded from elevations ranging from near sea level to 485 m (the highest station). Most frequently captured amongst leaf pack and from refuges under stones where the substrate was stony and the current was fast. Also observed at lentic environments, e.g., the concrete swimming pool below Dark View Falls. Small individuals were found among tree roots trailing in the river. *A. innocous* reaches high densities in mountain torrents above waterfalls, areas which exclude predatory fish. An ambulatory species, they use their robust legs to move over the stream bed and swim only when disturbed (Fryer, 1977b). Coat *et al.* (2011) report that the preferred current velocity is 50 cm/s and depth of 35 cm.

FEEDING AND DIET: The diet consists of detritus produced by the breakdown of forest leaves (Fryer, 1977a). *Atya innocous* has two methods of feeding.
1. Sweeping and scraping - The brush like bristles at the end of the first and second periopods open to resemble an inverted umbrella. Side bristles close the gap between the main bristles. These structures can be opened over a stone then closed to capture detritus from the surface which is then be transported to the mouth.

2. Filter feeding - The shrimp faces into the current and opens the bristles on the ends of all four front periopods (Figure 40). When food particles are carried into the "umbrella", it is closed and the food is then transported to the mouth (Fryer, 1977b).

LIFE CYCLE AND REPRODUCTION: Amphydromous. Reproduction occurs in freshwater. Mating takes place soon after the female has moulted and the carapace is still soft. Males are attracted by pheromones released by newly moulted females. At mating, the male transfers a spermatophore into a receptacle on the female's abdomen. After fertilization, thousands of eggs are released between the cephalothorax and abdomen and cemented in a mass between the pleopods by a glandular secretion (Felgenhauer and Abele, 1982). The eggs remain under the female's abdomen until hatching. During brooding, the female fans the eggs by rhythmically beating the pleopods to remove pathogens and oxygenate them. On hatching, vigorous movement of the pleopods assist release of the larvae into the environment. Hatching occurs most often at night. Newly hatched larvae are carried by the current to the ocean. Laboratory experiments by Hunte (1977) found that larvae did not survive in freshwater and that optimum survival occurred at a salinity of 30°/$_{oo}$. Nine ovigerous females were recorded in the survey in March. The minimum recorded carapace length of an ovigerous female was 14mm. Reproduction is believed to take place nearly year round (Horton and Hobbs, 1982).

CONSERVATION STATUS (IUCN): Least concern (De Grave, 2013).

Figure 40. *Atya innocous* filter feeding facing into the current. **(Photo S. Hornsey)**

IMPORTANCE TO FISHERIES: Commonly targeted by river fishermen. The most common methods of fishing are the traditional crayfish basket (Figure 41) and fishing by hand. "Bookie" are caught for human consumption and for use as bait in sea fishing.

Figure 41 (i). A traditional crayfish basket.

Figure 41 (ii). A catch of bookies.

Atya scabra (Leach, 1816)

COMMON NAME: Camacuto Shrimp

VINCENTIAN NAME: Bookie, Army Bookie

Figure 42. Male *Atya scabra*.

STATUS: Native

RECORDED IN LITERATURE FOR ST. VINCENT: Harrison and Rankin (1976). Guilding (1823) noted that *Atya scaber* (original spelling) "occurs in great numbers in mountain streams" in St.Vincent. However, Horton and Hobbs (1982) suggest that the species identified by Guilding was most likely to be the more common *A. innocous*.

OCCURRENCE IN THE ST. VINCENT SURVEY: A less frequently occurring species. Found at one location, station 14 on the Lower Camacarbou River. Nine specimens were examined. *A. scabra* is also reported to be a less common species than *A. innocous* in Dominica (Chance and Hobbs, 1969).

DESCRIPTION: Similar in general appearance to *Atya innocous*. Chelea of the first and second periopods end in brush-like structures. Walking legs are very robust: an ambulatory species. Differs from *A. innocous* in that the 3rd, 4th and 5th walking legs are covered in larger spines. The merus, carpus and propodus of 3rd pereiopod are much enlarged. The carapace is covered with hairlike structures which can be felt when handling the animal.
Males are larger than females with the maximum total length of males being 98 mm and females being 56 mm (Holthuis 1980). The specimens in this survey had a carapace length between 14.4 mm and 30.8 mm. The maximum carapace length noted by Holthuis (1980) was 39 mm.
Two colour phases are described by Chance and Hobbs (1969) a dark green and brown (Figure 42).

RANGE: – West Africa, from Liberia to Angola, and the Cape Verde Islands. Antilles, from Cuba south to Trinidad and Curacao, and Mexico to Brazil. Noted from the Pacific slope of Panama (Horton and Hobbs, 1982).

HABITAT: – The survey location where *A. scabra* was found was a shallow (<30 cm) riffle over a stony substrate at an elevation of 44 m. This species has been recorded from similar habitats in Dominica (Chance and Hobbs, 1969) and Brazil (Galvão and Bueno, 2000).
Coat *et al.* (2011) report that *A. scabra* prefers a current velocity of 63cm/s and a depth of 26 cm. Fishermen report that though not a widespread species, *A. scabra* can be locally abundant in St. Vincent. Grandgirard *et al.* (2014), cited in Lim (2002) as describing this species as gregarious.

FEEDING AND DIET: Feeds in a similar manner as described for *A. innocous*. Tank observations by Fryer (1977a) demonstrate that *A. scabra* feeds comparatively less by scraping and more by filtering than *A. innocous*. Fryer (1977a) suggest that differences in the feeding structures that give *A. innocous* the ability to feed effectively using both scraping and filtering allow *A. innocous* to utilise a greater variety of habitats than *A. scabra* which is confined to areas of swift current which facilitate filter feeding.

LIFE CYCLE AND REPRODUCTION: Amphidromous. Reproduction is similar to *Atya innocous*. Ovigerous females were found in all months of the year in Brazil (Galvão and Bueno, 2000). Reproductive females carry an average of 8343 eggs (Herrera-Correal *et al.*, 2013). Laboratory studies by Cruz-Soltero and Alston (1992) found best hatching success in fresh water: 82% larval mortality occurred within 6 hours in fresh water, but 100% larval survival at 30°/₀₀ suggesting hatching occurs in freshwater and larval development in an estuarine or marine environment. No ovigerous females were found in the present study.

CONSERVATION STATUS (IUCN): Least Concern worldwide (De Grave *et al.*, 2013). In Northeast Brazil, the species is considered near threatened due to significant declines in population and local extinctions attributed to water removal and diversion for electricity generation and water supply for domestic and industrial purposes (Barros-Alves *et al.*, 2021).

IMPORTANCE TO FISHERIES: Captured by river fishermen in St. Vincent using a basket and by hand. Historically, of local economic importance in Venezuela, Brazil and Puerto Rico. A subsistence fishery exists in Mexico (Holthuis, 1980). *A. scabra* is heavily fished by artisanal subsistence fishermen of Ivory Coast (Kadjo *et al.*, 2016).

Micratya poeyi (Guerérin-Méneville, 1855)

COMMON NAME: Caribbean dwarf filter shrimp

VINCENTIAN NAME: Bookie

Figure 43. *Micratya poeyi*.

STATUS: Native

RECORDED IN LITERATURE FOR ST. VINCENT: Harrison and Rankin (1976).

OCCURRENCE IN THE ST. VINCENT SURVEY: recorded from 8 stations in the present survey: 1, 2, 6, 16, 20, 21, 31, 34. Thirty-nine specimens were collected.

DESCRIPTION: A small species, which is very similar to the larger *Atya* species in general morphology (Figure 43). Robust walking legs: an ambulatory species. Differentiated from other *Atya* species by the presence of teeth on the dorsal surface of the rostrum (Figure 44).

Figure 44. Dorsal Rostral teeth of *Micratya poeyi*.

Chance and Hobbs (1969) identified three colour patterns in specimens from Dominica; tan vertical bands (Figure 45), tan dorsal median stripe, unbanded dark. All colour morphs were observed in St. Vincent.

Figure 45. Illustration of the colour patterns in *Micratya poeyi*. **(Artist Madeleine Smith)**

RANGE: – Atlantic slope of Costa Rica, Panama and Venezuela. The Antilles from Cuba south to Trinidad (De Grave, 2013).

HABITAT: – Found at foot hill torrent (1), mountain torrent (6) and headwater stream (1) stations with high flow. Most often captured with a dip net from amongst trailing tree roots, and loose gravel. Recorded from a wide range of elevations from 33 m to 485 m (the highest station). Chance and Hobbs (1969) note that this species prefers swift current.

FEEDING AND DIET: Scrapes and filter feeds in a similar manner to other *Atya spp.* (Fryer, 1977a). Leaves cover to feed at night.

LIFE CYCLE AND REPRODUCTION: Amphidromous. Ovigerous females are observed in freshwater, but larvae survive best in salinities of 32°/$_{oo}$, suggesting that larval development occurs in a marine environment (Hunte, 1977). Larvae develop in marine conditions for 30-50 days before returning to freshwater as post larvae (US Forest Service Page). Chance and Hobbs (1969) suggest reproduction occurs year-round. In the present survey 22 ovigerous females were collected between February and April.

CONSERVATION STATUS (IUCN): Least concern (De Grave, 2013)

IMPORTANCE TO FISHERIES: Too small to be targeted by river fishermen. This species is kept in aquaria by hobbyists.

Jonga serrei (Bouvier, 1909)

COMMON NAME: Basket shrimp

VINCENTIAN NAME: Bookie

Figure 46. Illustration of *Jonga serri*. (Artist Madeleine Smith)

STATUS: Native

RECORDED IN LITERATURE FOR ST. VINCENT: Harrison and Rankin (1976).

OCCURRENCE IN THE ST. VINCENT SURVEY: Recorded from 5 stations in the St. Vincent survey: 17, 26, 28, 32, 35. Twenty-four specimens were collected.

DESCRIPTION: A small species, which is very similar to the larger *Atyid* species in general morphology but less robust (Figure 46). The carapace length of specimens examined in the survey ranged from 2.2 to 5.7 mm, with an average CL of 4.2 mm. The maximum total length observed by Fryer (1977a) in Dominica was 24.8 mm.
Chelea of the first and second periopods end in brush-like structures. Walking legs are long and slender adapted to "tip toe" over the surface (Fryer, 1977a). The pleopods are well developed and it swims well (Fryer, 1977a). The rostrum is relatively long and bears ventral teeth (Figure 47). Colour patterns vary. Females with a median stripe and transverse bands were observed by Chance and Hobbs (1969).

Figure 47. Ventral rostral teeth in *Jonga serrei*.

RANGE: – Mexico. Central America - Atlantic slopes of Costa Rica, Panama. Venezuela. Antilles from Cuba south to Trinidad (de Grave, 2012).

HABITAT: – Recorded from semi-estuarine pool stations (4) and one pool in a foot hill torrent (1) station. All stations were at an elevation of less than 15 m and were within a few metres of the sea. These stations were all characterised by low flow and a sandy or muddy substrate. Fryer (1977a) suggests that the less robust body of *J. serrei* is best adapted to near lentic conditions. This species was always captured amongst emergent marginal vegetation.

FEEDING AND DIET: Sweeps diatoms and detritus from the surface of plants and the substrate (Fryer, 1977b).

LIFE CYCLE AND REPRODUCTION: Amphidromous (Fievet *et al.*, 2001). In the present survey, ovigerous females were recorded in March and June. A large proportion of specimens examined were ovigerous females.

CONSERVATION STATUS (IUCN): Least concern (de Grave *et al.*, 2012).

IMPORTANCE TO FISHERIES: This species is too small to be targeted by river fishermen.

Family: XIPHOCARIDIDAE

Xiphocaris elongata (Guerérin-Méneville, 1855)

COMMON NAME: Yellow nosed shrimp, Salpiche, Piquine

VINCENTIAN NAME: Jumper

STATUS: Native

RECORDED IN LITERATURE FOR ST. VINCENT: Harrison and Rankin (1976).

Figure 48. *Xiphocaris elongata*.

OCCURRENCE IN THE ST. VINCENT SURVEY: Recorded from stations 25, 29, 31, and 36. Fifteen specimens were examined.

DESCRIPTION: A medium sized slender and slightly built shrimp (Figure 48). Maximum size 69 mm (Fryer 1977a). In the present survey CL ranged from 3 to 14 mm, with an average CL of 9.3 mm. No brush-like hairs on the dactylus of the 1st and 2nd pereopods which end in pinchers. The eye is well developed. The antennal flagellum long. Walking legs long and slight (Figure 48). Observed to walk "tip toe" with only the claw tips of the dactyli touching the substrate Fryer (1977a). The pleopods are well developed and facilitate effective swimming. The body is translucent and the internal organs visible. A purple stripe is visible on the lateral posterior area of the carapace (Chance and Hobbs, 1969). The rostrum is very long: the dorsal surface is finely toothed in the rear section only; the ventral surface has very fine teeth along its length and is marked with a distinctive orange yellow band. A long rostrum is an antipredator device in this species. *X. elongata* found in rivers where predatory fish are present, have longer rostra than where such predators are absent. In tank experiments, mountain mullet preferentially predated and more successfully attacked individuals with a short rostrum (Ocasio-Torres *et al.*, 2015).

RANGE: – Antilles, Cuba south to Trinidad. Colombia and Venezuela (de Grave, 2013)

HABITAT: – Recorded from 3 mountain torrent stations and 1 foothill torrent station. All specimens examined were adults and captured from pools in smaller streams. Adults were found at altitudes ranging from 64 to 380m. Juveniles were not observed in the present survey but were previously recorded amongst emergent vegetation at the semi-estuarine pool of the Buccament River. The use of different habitats by juveniles and adults was noted in Dominica (Chance and Hobbs, 1969). A study by Johnson and Covich (2000) revealed that *X. elongata* was much more active nocturnally and made greater use of shallow and low current velocity areas at night.

FEEDING AND DIET: A detritivore. The chela (pincers) on the first and second walking legs are used to pick up detritus from the substrate or pinch pieces of sunken forest leaves. In a study using stable isotope analysis (Coat *et al.*, 2009), the diet of *X. elongata* was estimated to be 62% leaf and fruit detritus, 27% algae and 11% biofilm. Fryer (1977a) found "plant fragments of terrestrial origin" in the guts of *X. elongata*. A tank experiment by March *et al.* (2001) demonstrated that *Xiphocaris* was more effective at breaking down forest leaves than *Atya* or *Macrobrachium* species. In the upper reaches, where adult *Xiphocaris* are most common, the forest trees shade the river, reducing in stream photosynthetic production. In mountain forests, leaves that fall from trees are more significant input than production by producers in stream. Shredding of leaves by *Xiphocaris* reduces detritus particles to a size accessible to other detritivores that feed by filtering or scraping (Crowl *et al.*, 2006).

LIFE CYCLE AND REPRODUCTION: Amphidromous. No ovigerous females were found between February and April in the present survey.

CONSERVATION STATUS (IUCN): Least concern (De Grave 2013).

IMPORTANCE TO FISHERIES: Caught incidentally by river fishermen in St. Vincent. This species is difficult to catch as it deploys the cardioid escape reaction when touched. This involves the rapid flexing of the abdomen resulting in powerful backward movement which can carry the shrimp out of the water.

Family: PALAEMONIDAE

Macrobrachium acanthurus (Wiegmann, 1836)

COMMON NAME: Cinnamon River Prawn

VINCENTIAN NAME: Swampy, Salt Pond Crayfish, Yambou Crayfish

STATUS: Native

RECORDED IN LITERATURE FOR ST. VINCENT: Harrison and Rankin (1976).

OCCURRENCE IN THE ST. VINCENT SURVEY: Recorded from five stations: 23, 26, 32, 35, 37. Fifty-five specimens were examined.

DESCRIPTION: A large species, with largest total length observed by Valencia and Campos (2007) in Colombia reported to be 167.2 mm. In the present survey, CL ranged from 10 mm to 50 mm, with an average CL of 23.4 mm. Rostrum large, extending beyond the scaphocerite and curved upwards in large specimens (Figure 49). The rostrum has 8-12 dorsal teeth and 4-7 ventral teeth. The 2nd pair of pereopods are long, slender and nearly equal in size. The eyes are prominent and large (Valencia and Campos, 2007; Chance and Hobbs, 1969). There are three prominent purple markings on the ventral part of the carapace resembling the figure and letter combination of '**13Y**' (Figure 49). Two colour patterns were observed in St. Vincent, pale pink/grey and a cinnamon form.

Figure 49. *Macrobrachium acanthurus*.

RANGE: A widely distributed species. Atlantic drainages from North Carolina USA, Gulf of Mexico, Central America and South America to Southern Brazil (de Grave, 2013). Records of *M. acanthurus* from the Pacific slope of Central and South America have now been confirmed as a genetically different species, *Macrobrachium tenellum* (Pileggi *et al.*, 2014).

HABITAT: – In the St. Vincent survey this species was recorded exclusively from semi-estuarine pool stations. Four of five stations were on the leeward side of the island. Most frequently captured amongst emergent vegetation over a muddy substrate and low flow conditions.

Coat *et al.* (2011) report that the preferred current velocity is 6cm/s and depth 34cm. All stations where this species was found in St. Vincent were near sea level and only a few metres from the sea. *M. acanthurus* is reported from a similar habitat in Dominica (Chance and Hobbs, 1969) and Guadeloupe (Coat *et al.*, 2011). In large continental rivers in Venezuela, with long low gradient lower reaches, adults have been reported 30 km from the sea but not from elevations greater than 20 m (Gamba, 1982). Bertini *et al.* (2014) report this species 300 km from the river mouth in Brazil. Usually reported from turbid water with a muddy substrate but can occur in clear water with stony substrate (Gamba, 1982).

FEEDING AND DIET: Omnivorous. In a study of the stomach contents of *M. acanthurus* from a costal lagoon in Brazil the main item in the diet, by occurrence was detritus, followed in order by, insects, algae, fish, annelid worms, crustaceans and mollusks (Albertoni *et al.*, 2003). Lafrancois *et al.* (2011) reported that biofilm comprised 13% of the diet. A study of the source of the diet using stable isotopes analysis found food from animal sources to be most important in juveniles and plant detritus in adults (Coat *et al.*, 2009).

LIFE CYCLE AND REPRODUCTION: 1 ovigerous female found during the St. Vincent survey in April.

Amphidromous (Fievet *et al.*, 2001). Reproduction takes place in fresh or brackish water (Fukada 2016). The female broods a large number (133-5568) of comparatively small eggs (63.25 μm) (Valencia and Campos, 2007; Mejía-Ortíz, 2001). Reproduction occurs year-round but peaks in the wet season in Brazil (Mejía-Ortíz, 2001).

Newly hatched larvae can survive for 10 days in freshwater, but require brackish water of salinity 15-20$°/_{oo}$ in order to develop into post larvae (Choudhury, 1971). The larvae development lasts 30-40 days. Bertini *et al.* (2014) suggest that "estuarine conditions represent an obligatory requisite for successful development in *M. acanthurus*". It has been suggested that reproductive female *M acanthurus* migrate down river in order to reduce the distance that larvae must drift in order to reach appropriate salinity conditions for development. However, no evidence for migration by females was found (Bretini, 2014).

The only brackish habitat in St. Vincent is the semi-estuarine pool. Limited observations of salinity of the semi-estuarine pool of the Buccament River (Station 26), were made using a Westover RHS-10ATC refractometer in June (wet season). On this occasion, the salinity was found to be only slightly brackish with a maximum salinity of 11 $°/_{oo}$ within 10 m of the river mouth and 0 $°/_{oo}$ at 15 m behind the river mouth. Preliminary results suggest that the salinity of the semi-estuarine pool is too low for the successful development of *M. acanthurus* larvae in this habitat. In St. Vincent, adult *M acanthurus* are restricted to the semi-estuarine pool, larvae hatched in this location drift to the river mouth within tens of metres. Bell and Browne (1995) propose that low salinity systems exist as a result of freshwater discharge from rivers into the sea and that the less dense freshwater persists, lying above the more saline oceanic water slowly mixing to provide an intermediate salinity suited for development of larval amphidromous taxa.

CONSERVATION STATUS (IUCN): Least concern (de Grave, 2013).

Coat et al. (2011) found *M. acanthurus* to be one of the most susceptible fish/shrimp species to the bioaccumulation of organochloride pesticides in Guadeloupe.

IMPORTANCE TO FISHERIES: Targeted by river fishermen in St. Vincent, fishing by hand and basket. Effort is limited by the restricted area in which this species is found here.

An important artisanal fishery in Mexico, Venezuela and Brazil (Holthuis, 1980). Sold in local markets in Brazil where it is the second most important species of freshwater shrimp to fisheries after *M. carcinus* (Almedia *et al.*, 2008).

The large size and culinary quality of *M. acanthurus* attracted interest in the species potential for aquaculture, particularly in Latin America. García-Guerrero (2013) reviewed several studies to determine the dietary and physiological requirements of *M. acanthurus* for aquaculture. Aspects of the culture of *M. acanthurus* are more expensive than the widely cultured *Macrobrachium rosenbergii* (Hagood and Willis, 1976).

Macrobrachium carcinus (Linnaeus, 1758)

COMMON NAME: Big Claw River Shrimp

VINCENTIAN NAME: River Lobster

STATUS: Native

RECORDED IN LITERATURE FOR ST. VINCENT: Chance and Hobbs (1969)

OCCURRENCE IN THE ST. VINCENT SURVEY: Recorded from 10 stations: 2,5,7,14,15,26,27,28,29,38. Twenty-five specimens were examined.

DESCRIPTION: A very large species, "the largest species of American shrimp" (Chance and Hobbs, 1969). The maximum total length is reported as 233 mm in males and 170 mm in females (Holthuis, 1980). In the St. Vincent survey, the largest specimen recorded was a male with carapace length of 84 mm and total length of 210 mm.

Tip of rostrum is upturned, 11-16 ventral teeth, 3-4 dorsal teeth. Second pereiopods of males near equal in size and form. There is a prominent tooth on the cutting edge of both the fixed and movable finger of the second pereiopod (Figure 51). Eyes well developed. The only shrimp species found localy with longitudinal bands on the abdomen. Colour in adults: carapace dark brown, abdomen dark brown with tan longitudinal stripes (Figure 50), while in juveniles the longitudinal stripes are more defined and lighter in colour (Figure 52). Eyes well developed.

Figure 50. *Macrobrachium carcinus* Adult male. (The tip of the fixed finger on the right 2nd pereiopod is broken in this specimen.)

Figure 51. Teeth on the cutting edge of the finger of the second pereiopod of *M. carcinus*.

Figure 52. Juvenile *M. carcinus* with prominent longitudinal stripes.

RANGE: – Atlantic drainages from Florida USA, Mexico, Central America and South America south to Southern Brazil. The Antilles (de Grave, 2013). Records of *M. carcinus* from the Pacific slope of Central and South America have now been confirmed as a genetically different species *Macrobrachium americanum (*Pileggi *et al*., 2014).

HABITAT: – A widespread species in St. Vincent. Recorded from 10 stations in a range of habitats: semi-estuarine pool (1), foot hill torrent (4) and mountain torrent (5) stations. This species was found in large and small rivers; most were caught at stations on major rivers (5). Usually found under the cover of large boulders in strong current. Recorded from elevations ranging from near sea level to 256 m above sea level.
Coat *et al*. (2011) report the preferred current velocity is 50 cm/s and depth of 43 cm for *M. carcinus*. Adults found in freshwater (Holthuis, 1980). In Venezuela, juveniles are reported from near the river mouth and adults higher in the river system (Gamba, 1982).

FEEDING AND DIET: Omnivorous, with a significant carnivorous component. In a study of the stomach contents of *M. carcinus* from the Amazon River, detritus (plant and animal) was the largest component of the diet followed, in order, by plant fragments and crustaceans (Lima *et al*., 2014). A study by Coat *et al*. (2009) using stable isotope analysis found the carnivorous component of the diet to be more important: 66% consisting of molluscs, juveniles shrimp, detritivorous shrimp and omnivorous fish; and 34% consisting of plant detritus, biofilm and algae. More active at night.

LIFE CYCLE AND REPRODUCTION: In the St. Vincent survey, 2 ovigerous females were recorded in June.
Amphidromous (Fievet *et al*., 2001). Reproduction takes place in freshwater. Larvae drift down stream. In Costa Rica, Gamba (1982) recorded ovigerous females in all months but reproduction peaked from June to October, corresponding with the wet season. In Costa Rica, Lara (2009) recorded ovigerous females between 120 and 190 mm total length, with average fecundity of 98,749 eggs. No downstream migration of reproductive females has been observed (Bertini *et al*., 2014). Larvae require brackish water, 14-16°/$_{oo}$ salinity in which to develop (Choudhury, 1971a). Larval development takes 45-90 days. As only a limited estuarine environment exists in St. Vincent, larval development in this context probably occurs in low salinity environments at sea produced by freshwater runoff.

CONSERVATION STATUS (IUCN): Least concern (De Grave 2013). In Brazil this species is included on the national Red List of Threatened Species due to decline in numbers due to: overfishing, habitat destruction, pollution and dam construction (Almeida *et al.*, 2008).

IMPORTANCE TO FISHERIES: The shrimp species most targeted by river fishermen due to their high economic and culinary value. Fishing for river lobster is more effective at night. Fishing methods and gear used include: fishing by hand, spear (Figure 53), hook and line and basket in descending order of importance. A specialised method of hook and line fishing is used to catch river lobsters using the gear shown in Figure 54. A hook, usually baited with crayfish, is fixed lightly to the end of the rod. The hook is often made from a bent needle. The rod is used to push the baited hook under cover suspected of holding river lobster. If the river lobster is felt taking the bait and removing the hook from the end of the rod, the fisherman pauses until the hook is taken into the mouth. The river lobster is then retrieved using sufficient pressure to remove it from cover while not pulling the hook out of the river lobster's delicate mouth parts. This method of fishing for lobster was observed by Chance and Hobbs (1969) in Dominica and Holthuis (1980) in Curaçao.

Figure 53. A river lobster captured at the semi-estuarine pool of the Buccament River (station 26) by expert river fisherman, Shem Gaymes using a spear gun he made himself. **(Photo S. Hornsey)**

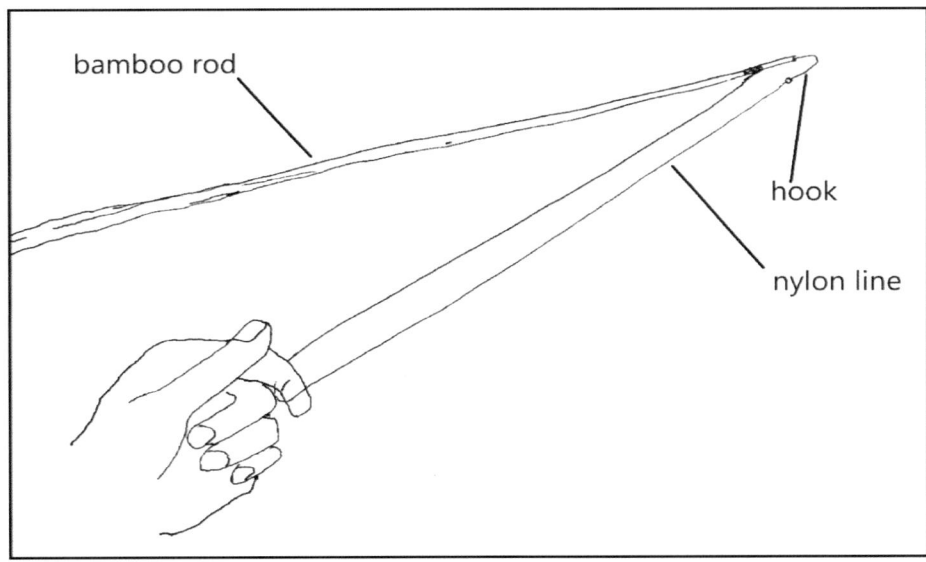

Figure 54. Specialised hook and line method used to catch *Macrobrachium carcinus*, river lobster.

Important fisheries for *M.carcinus* exist in Mexico, Venezuela, Suriname and Brazil (Holthuis, 1980). It is the most exploited freshwater shrimp species in Latin America. However few fisheries statistics are recorded (Garcia-Guerrero, 2013). Studies to investigate the potential of this species for aquaculture have been carried out in the USA, Barbados (Holthuis, 1980) and Latin America (Garcia-Gerrero, 2013).

Macrobrachium crenulatum Holthuis, 1950

Little research has been done on this species.

COMMON NAME: No English common name.

VINCENTIAN NAME: Glass Bottle, Bottle Man, Madras, Red Tail, Yellow Tail, Blue Bean, Blue Man

STATUS: Native

RECORDED IN LITERATURE FOR ST. VINCENT: No records of this species in the literature for St. Vincent. However, specimens collected here are lodged at the Naturalis Biodiversity Center, Netherlands (GBIF, 2023)

OCCURRENCE IN THE ST. VINCENT SURVEY: Recorded from 12 stations: 6, 7, 9, 10, 11, 19, 20, 23, 25, 31, 32, 34. Thirty specimens were examined.

Figure 55. *Macrobrachium crenulatum* male.

Figure 56. Illustration of *M. crenulatum*. (Artist Madeleine Smith)

STATUS: Native

RECORDED IN LITERATURE FOR ST. VINCENT: No records of this species in the literature for St. Vincent. However specimens collected here are lodged at the Naturalis Biodiversity Center, Netherlands (GBIF, 2023)

OCCURRENCE IN THE ST. VINCENT SURVEY: Recorded from 12 stations: 6, 7, 9, 10, 11, 19, 20, 23, 25, 31, 32, 34. Thirty specimens were examined.

DESCRIPTION: A medium sized species. In the St. Vincent survey, CL ranged from 18.3 to 34.2 mm, with an average CL of 20.4 mm. Chance and Hobbs (1969) report the maximum carapace length in males from Dominica to be 29.4 mm. The maximum total length observed from Colombia was 81 mm (Valencia and Campos, 2007). Rostrum armed with 11-14 dorsal and 4-6 ventral teeth (Figures

55 and 56). Tip of rostrum is not upturned (Chance and Hobbs, 1969). Second pereiopods are unequal in shape and size (Figure 55) Cutting surface of the fingers of the pincers thickly covered in hair like structures. Palm with rows of prominent spines (Valencia and Campos, 2007). Colour in males: general colouration dark blue/black. There is a pale patch on the posterior part of the 3rd abdominal somite. The coxa, top segment of the walking legs, are pale yellow/red. The tail is conspicuously coloured, the telson is red and the uropods are red with yellow outer margins (Chance and Hobbs, 1969; Hunte, 1979). Females are less conspicuously marked.

RANGE: – Mexico, Costa Rica (Pileggi *et al.*, 2014), Panama (Torati *et al.*, 2011), Colombia (Valencia and Campos, 2007), Venezuela (Pileggi *et al.*, 2014), Jamaica, Hispaniola, Puerto Rico the Lesser Antilles, Trinidad (Hunte, 1979).

HABITAT: – Recorded in the St. Vincent survey from semi-estuarine pool stations (2) but was most frequently found in foot hill torrent (4) and mountain torrent (6) stations. Found in riffles, pools and shelters amongst leaf pack and under stones. Coat et al. (2011) report that *M. crenulatum* favours current velocity of 28 cm/s and depth of 65 cm.

FEEDING AND DIET: Omnivorous. Stable isotope analysis estimated the diet of *M. crenulatum* to be 38% allochthonous sources (plant and fruit detritus), 27% autochthonous (filamentous green algae and biofilm) and 36% from animal sources (Coat *et al.*, 2009). Reported to prey on guppies in Trinidad (Egset, 2011).

LIFE CYCLE AND REPRODUCTION: 1 ovigerous female, 22.5 mm carapace length was collected in March during the St. Vincent survey.
Amphidromous (Kikkert *et al.*, 2009). Chance and Hobbs (1969) collected ovigerous females in Dominica over several months suggesting a prolonged breeding season.

CONSERVATION STATUS (IUCN): Least Concern (De Grave, 2013).

IMPORTANCE TO FISHERIES: Caught by river fishermen when fishing for crayfish but not specifically targeted. Gear most often used is the crayfish basket also caught by hand.

Macrobrachium faustinum (de Saussure, 1857)

COMMON NAME: Caribbean Long Arm Shrimp

VINCENTIAN NAME: Buss finger, Grass Tail

STATUS: Native

RECORDED IN LITERATURE FOR ST. VINCENT: Harrison and Rankin (1976b).

OCCURRENCE IN THE ST. VINCENT SURVEY: Recorded from 13 stations: 9, 11, 13, 14, 17, 19, 23, 26, 27, 29, 33, 36, 37. Thirty-four specimens were examined.

Figure 57. *Macrobrachium faustinum* male.

DESCRIPTION: A smaller *Macrobrachium* species. The maximum carapace length found in the survey was 21 mm and maximum total length 56 mm. Chance and Hobbs (1969) report a maximum carapace length of about 18 mm. The rostrum is near straight, with the tip turned slightly downwards; 12-15 teeth on the dorsal and 2-4 teeth on the ventral surfaces. The second pereiopods are of different shape and size (Chance and Hobbs, 1969; Valencia and Campos, 2007). The palm of the larger pereiopod is covered in dense, soft fur, hence the local name "buss finger" (Figure 57). Colour: near translucent; the body is straw coloured.

RANGE: – Florida, the Antilles, Venezuela and Colombia (de Grave, 2013). Bowles *et al*. (2009) suggests that this species may be introduced to Florida.

HABITAT: – Recorded from semi-estuarine pools (5), foothill torrents (5) and mountain torrent (3) stations. A common and widely distributed species in St. Vincent. Most frequently found in slow flow areas, and from among emergent vegetation, but also in riffles. Large numbers were found amongst decomposing *Sargassum* in the semi-estuarine pool at Spring, Biabou (station 17). Most common in the lower reaches. Robinson et al. (2002) report adults being found in fresh and brackish water. The preferred current velocity is 13 cm/s and depth 22 cm (Coat *et al*., 2011).

FEEDING AND DIET: Omnivorous. Stable isotope analysis estimated the diet of *M. faustinum* to be 25% allochthonous sources (plant and fruit detritus), 33% autochthonous (filamentous green algae and biofilm) and 40% from animal sources (Coat *et al*., 2009). Biofilm is estimated to comprise 16% of the diet (Lefrancois, 2011).

LIFE CYCLE AND REPRODUCTION: Two ovigerous females were captured in the month of June during the St. Vincent survey.
Amphidromous (Fievet *et al*., 2001). Larvae develop at sea for 95 days before returning to rivers as post larvae (Hunte and Mahon, 1983). In Jamaica, Hunte and Mahon (2008) report that breeding takes place throughout the year, but peaks between June and November.

CONSERVATION STATUS (IUCN): Least concern (De Grave, 2013)

Coat *et al.* (2011) found *M. faustinum* to be one of the most susceptible fish/shrimp species to the bioaccumulation of organochloride pesticides in Guadeloupe.

IMPORTANCE TO FISHERIES: A small species caught when fishing for crayfish but not specifically targeted in St. Vincent.

Hunte and Mahon (1983) report a significant artisanal subsistence and recreational trap fishery for *M. faustinum* in Jamaica and performed an assessment of this fishery using a yield per recruit model. This study is the only example in the literature of an attempt to perform a formal fisheries assessment on a river fishery in the Caribbean. They concluded that fishing mortality (the fraction of the population expected to be killed by fishing for a given unit of time) was low (F=0.15) and that the fishery could support an increase in yield with a small increase in fishing effort. However, if fishing mortality were increased the mean size of the shrimp caught would decrease. As *M. faustinum* is already a small species reduction in size of the shrimp caught would likely incentivise a reduction in fishing effort – the fishery would therefore be self-regulating. Growth overfishing (catching the shrimp before they reach their full growth potential) even at high levels of exploitation would not likely occur as *M. faustinum* reproduce young and produce large numbers of eggs.

Macrobrachium heterochirus (Weigmann, 1836)

COMMON NAME: Cascade River Prawn

VINCENTIAN NAME: Colonaire Crayfish, Bamboo Crayfish, Malatar, Antigua

STATUS: Native

RECORDED IN LITERATURE FOR ST. VINCENT: Chance and Hobbs (1969).

OCCURRENCE IN THE ST. VINCENT SURVEY: Recorded from 16 stations: 2, 6, 8, 9, 10, 12, 18, 20, 21, 24, 25, 27, 29, 31, 34, 37. Fifty-six specimens were examined.

DESCRIPTION: A medium sized species. In the St. Vincent survey, the maximum carapace length was 30 mm and the maximum total length 95 mm. Holthuis (1980) reports a maximum total length of 135 mm for males and 75 mm for females. Dorsal surface of the rostrum is somewhat curved with a slightly upturned tip; 10-13 teeth with the 3 or 4 posterior teeth larger and more widely spaced; 2-3 ventral rostral teeth. The second pereiopods are prominently elongated, equal in shape but not size, with a tubular palm. Colouration is light and dark brown with characteristic prominent dark brown/black transverse banding on the first three abdominal somites (Figures 58 and 59). **RANGE:** – Mexico, Central America south to Brazil. The Antilles (de Grave, 2013). Recorded in Florida USA, possibly introduced (Bowels *et al.*, 2000).

HABITAT: Found at semi-estuarine pool (3), foothill torrent (4), mountain torrent (8) and headwater stream (1) stations. Widely distributed in the survey. It was commonly present but not numerous at any location. Recorded at elevations, from near sea level to 484 m, the highest station in the survey. It was most often captured in riffles and runs over stony substrates.

Chance and Hobbs (1969) observed that this species was widespread in riffles and cascades along the stream gradient in Dominica. Coat *et al.* (2011) report a preference for current velocity of 66 cm/s and depth of 36 cm. Statistical analyses showed that *M. heterochirus* had a strong preference for locations with high current velocity in Guadeloupe (Grandgirard *et al.*, 2014). Meyer-Rochow *et al.* (1992) note physiological adaptation for night vision, suggesting that this species is nocturnal.

Figure 58. Illustration of *Macrobrachium heterochirus*, male. (Artist Madeline Smith)

Figure 59. *Macrobrachium heterochirus*, male.

FEEDING AND DIET: Omnivorous. Stable isotope analysis estimated the diet of *M. heterochirus* to be 33% allochthonous sources (plant and fruit detritus), 21% autochthonous (filamentous green algae and biofilm) and 38% from animal sources (Coat *et al.*, 2009).The proportion of biofilm in the diet is estimated to be 12% (Lefrancis *et al.*, 2010).

LIFE CYCLE AND REPRODUCTION: 1 ovigerous female was recorded in March in the St. Vincent survey.

Amphidromous (Fievet *et al.*, 2001). The reproductive process was observed in this species and is similar to other species of *Macrobrachium* (Ching and Velez, 1985). A male guards a newly moulted female. Courtship and mating occur 2-5 hours after moulting of the female before the new exoskeleton has hardened. The male eats the female's moulted exoskeleton. Courtship involves touching with the antennae and pereiopods. Mating occurs when the male grasps the female with the 2nd pereiopods and deposits a sperm sac between the base of the 4th and 5th pereiopods of the female. A few hours later, the female extrudes fertilized eggs into a brood chamber formed from gelatinous material between the pleopods. Oviposition takes place 5-24 hours after mating. Incubation lasts between 14 and 19 days and can take place in fresh or brackish water. A fecundity of 293-28512 and an increase in egg size with increased distance from the sea was found for *M. heterochirus* in Mexico (Mejia-Ortiz *et al.*, 2001). Brackish water is required for larval development (Almeida *et al.*, 2008).

CONSERVATION STATUS (IUCN): Least Concern (De Grave, 2013).

IMPORTANCE TO FISHERIES: Caught by river fishermen in St. Vincent using the crayfish basket. Holthuis (1980) reports a minor fishery for this species in Northern Brazil, where it is used for bait.

Infraorder: Brachyura – True Crabs

The species of freshwater and brackish water crabs recorded in the St. Vincent Survey are summarised in Table 6.

Table 6. An inventory of crab species identified during the survey.

Scientific Name	Vernacular Names	Common Name	St. Vincent Stations Where Species was Recorded	Total Number of Stations Where Species Occurred
Family PORTUNIDAE (Swimming Crabs)				
Callinectes sapidus	Cherigo	Blue Crab	26, 32	2
Family PSEUDOTHELPHUSIDAE				
Guinotia dentata	River Crab	Cyrique	2,15,16,20, 24,36	6
Family GRAPSIDAE (Shore crabs)				
Armases roberti	Jumby Crab	None	13,17,22	3
Family OCYPODIDAE	Ghost crabs & Fiddler crabs			
Uca Sp.	Fiddler crab	Fiddler Crab	22	1

Family: Portunidae

Callinectes sapidus Rathburn, 1896

COMMON NAME: Blue Crab

VINCENTIAN NAME: Cherigo

Figure 60. *Callinectes sapidus*, male.

STATUS: Native

RECORDED IN LITERATURE FOR ST. VINCENT: First record for St. Vincent.

Recorded as present in St. Vincent in Sealife Base (Palomares and Pauly, 2024) which cites Tavares (2003) as the source. However, this reference refers only to a general range for the species and does not refer to observations or museum collections containing *Callinectes sapidus* from St. Vincent and the Grenadines.
GBIF (2024) reports that *Callinectes sapidus* is present in St. Vincent and the Grenadines based on a data set derived from a paper by Mantelatto *et al.* (2020) "Checklist of decapod crustaceans from the coast of the São Paulo state...". The record refers to specimens captured from the São Vincente estuary on the Rio Branco Brazil this location is misattributed to St. Vincent and the Grenadines. There are no records of museum specimens of *Callinectes sapidus* from St. Vincent and the Grenadines in GBIF.

OCCURRENCE IN THE ST. VINCENT SURVEY: Recorded from stations 26 and 32 in the St. Vincent survey. Three specimens were examined.

DESCRIPTION: A large crab. One male with carapace width (CW) of 143 mm and one female with CW of 110 mm were seen in the survey. Maximum CW reported is 209 mm (Tavares 2003). The carapace is twice as broad as long with 9 lateral teeth, the outermost very long. The area between the eyes bears two triangular teeth (Figure 60). Chelipeds are almost equal. The rearmost pair of walking legs is flattened to form paddles that assist in swimming. In males the first pleopods are very long and reach the fourth thoracic sternite (Figure 61). The abdomen in males is T-shaped (Figure 61) and broad in females (Figure 62). Colouration of the carapace is dark brown/green. Pincers in males are blue (Figure 60) and orange in females (Figure 62).

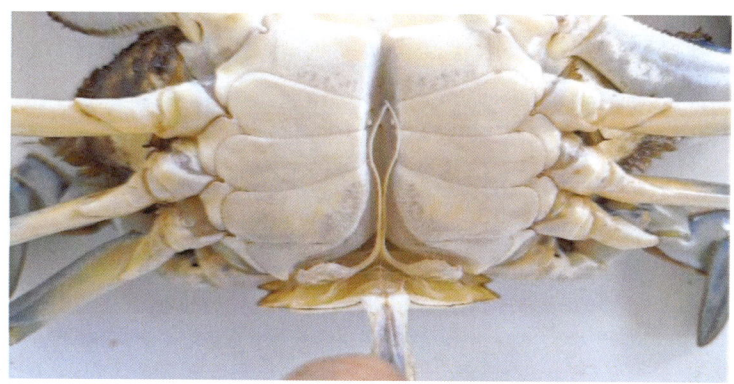

Figure 61. Ventral view of a male *C. sapidus* showing first pleopods.

Figure 62. Ventral view of a female *C. sapidus* with a wide apron and orange pincers.

RANGE: – From Nova Scotia to Argentina and the Antilles. Introduced to the North Sea, Mediterranean Sea, Black Sea and Japan (Tavares, 2003).

HABITAT: – Specimens were found at two semi-estuarine pool stations on the leeward side of the island where the substrate was muddy and the current velocity low.
Found in marine, brackish and freshwater environments (Tavares, 2003).

FEEDING AND DIET: Omnivorous but predominantly predatory. Blue crabs are opportunistic feeders and with a diet that varies according to the size of the crab and availability of food items over its large geographical range. A study of blue crab diet in Florida noted: juveniles <31 mm (CW) consumed bivalves, plant matter, ostracods and detritus; crabs 31-60 mm (CW) consumed fish, gastropods and xanthid crabs; crabs > 60 mm (CW) consumed bivalves, fish, xanthid crabs and blue crabs (Laughlin, 1982). Only larger crabs have pincers powerful enough to break open large bivalve shells. The blue crab is itself a prey item for fish and is a major component of the diet of the American eel in the USA, (Milliken and Williams, 1984).

LIFE CYCLE AND REPRODUCTION: Spawning occurs after the final moult of an adult female blue crab. Just before the moult, a male will cradle the female. Mating takes place after the moult, when the shell is soft. The male cradles the female until the new carapace hardens. The female stores the sperm until conditions are favourable. Stored sperm from this single mating will be used to fertilize all subsequent batches of eggs. Males remain in the estuarine environment, seeking females to mate with. After mating, females migrate from estuarine to more marine environments. Once in a suitable environment, fertilization is followed by the extrusion of between 700,000 and 2 million eggs, which are held in a mass under the female's abdomen (Milliken and Williams, 1984). After 14-17 days the eggs hatch into planktonic, zoea larvae which require salinity of >30 $^o/_{oo}$ for development. After 39-41 days the zoea develop into megalops larvae which settle on the substrate. The megalops stage lasts between 6 and 20 days. Megalops larvae and juvenile crabs migrate back into estuarine waters. Blue crabs reach maturity within 18 months (Davis, 2016).

CONSERVATION STATUS (IUCN): No reported status.

IMPORTANCE TO FISHERIES: Captured by river fishermen when available. However, its importance to fisheries in St. Vincen is limited by restricted available habitat.
A major coastal fishery occurs in the USA, focused on the Chesapeake Bay, where in the 1980s and 1990s, 50,000 tons/year were landed (Davis, 2016).

Family: Pseudothelphusidae

Guinotia dentata (Latreille, 1825)

COMMON NAME: Cyrique

VINCENTIAN NAME: River Crab

STATUS: Native

RECORDED IN LITERATURE FOR ST. VINCENT: Harrison and Rankin (1976) A museum specimen collected from St. Vincent is lodged at National Museum of Natural History, Smithsonian Institution (GBIF, 2023).

OCCURRENCE IN THE ST. VINCENT SURVEY: Recorded from 6 stations: 2, 15, 16, 20, 24, 34.

DESCRIPTION: A medium/large crab (Figure 63). Carapace widths of 18-88 mm were recorded in the St. Vincent survey. A maximum carapace width of 100 mm has been reported (Rodriguez 1982, cited in Prouzet and Christmas, 2021).

The carapace is roughly oval and has small regular teeth along the front edge. The carapace ranges from dark brown to yellow in colour between individuals. Chelipeds have an orange merus and carpus and white propodus and are of near equal size. Sexual dimorphism is apparent in the abdomen which is narrow in males and broad in females (Figures 64 and 65).

RANGE: – Endemic to the Lesser Antilles; Guadeloupe, Dominica, Martinique, St. Lucia, St. Vincent (Prouzet and Christmas, 2021). A single museum specimen collected in Tobago is lodged at the National Museum of Natural History, Smithsonian Institution (GBIF, 2023). Reported from Grenada, (iNaturalist, 2023).

Figure 63. *Guinotia dentata*. **(Photo by Fr. Mark De Silva)**

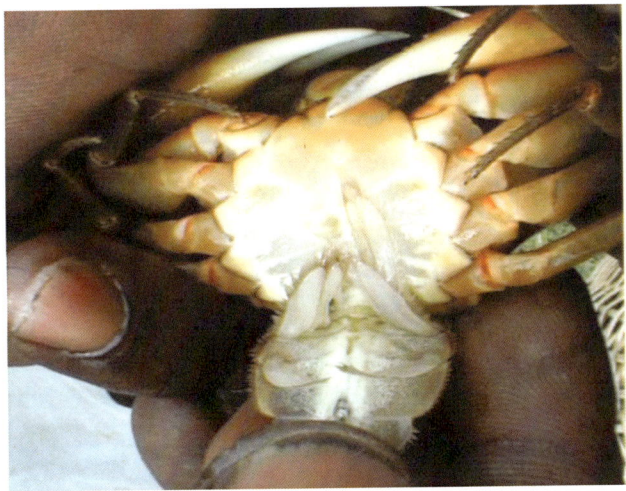

Figure 64. **Ventral view of a female** *Guinotia dentata*.

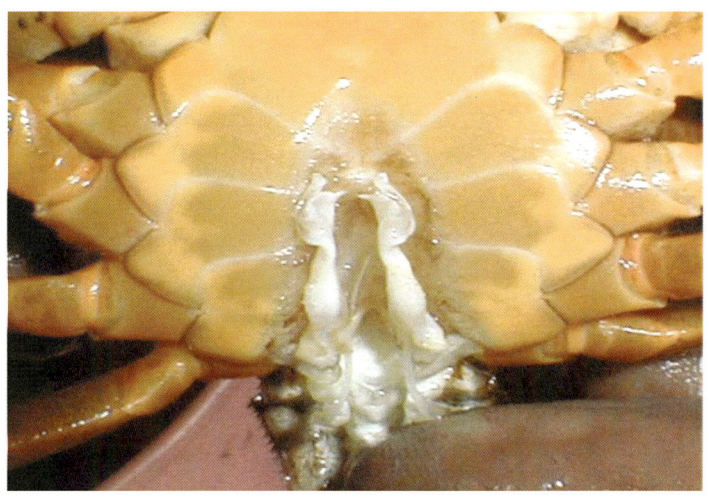

Figure 65. Ventral view of a male *Guinotia dentata.*

HABITAT: – Always recorded from stations classified as mountain torrents in the St. Vincent survey. Found at elevations ranging from 33 to 360 m. Likley to occur at higher elevations; Cumberlidge (2008) reports the maximum elevation as 457 m. Absent from the lower reaches (Chance and Hobbs, 1969). Found in riffles and pools, and amongst leaf packs. Most active at night (Miculka, 2009). Predominantly an aquatic species, though terrestrial environments in damp forested areas are used. *Guinotia dentata* digs burrows on land protected by tree roots or rocks. The entrance of the burrow is constructed to be wide enough to accommodate the width of the carapace so that the animal can view the environment from the burrow. The rest of tunnel is narrow and necessitates the crab to walk sideways in it (Miculka, 2009). Large adults and juveniles are most frequently observed in the river, and medium-sized animals in the terrestrial environment (Miculka, 2009).
Guinotia dentata is predated by the common black hawk, *Buteogallus anthracinus.*

FEEDING AND DIET: Omnivorous. Predominantly carnivorous, although detritus is also consumed (Prouzet and Christmas, 2021).

LIFE CYCLE AND REPRODUCTION: *Guinotia dentata* exhibits direct larval development (Burggren & McMahon, 1988). Juveniles hatch directly from the egg hence there are no larval stages requiring brackish water for development in this species. The female carries approximately 100 fertilized eggs under the abdomen until these hatch into miniature juvenile crabs. The juveniles continue to be brooded by the mother for some time before dispersing. The entire reproductive cycle takes place in freshwater (Prouzet and Christmas, 2021).

CONSERVATION STATUS (IUCN): Least concern (Cumberlidge, 2008)

IMPORTANCE TO FISHERIES: Targeted by river fishermen in St. Vincent

Family: Grapsidae

Armases roberti (H.Milne Edwards 1853)

COMMON NAME: None

VINCENTIAN NAME: Jumby Crab

STATUS: Native

RECORDED IN LITERATURE FOR ST. VINCENT: Harrison and Rankin (1976). A specimen collected in St. Vincent is lodged at the National Museum of Natural History, Smithsonian Institution (GBIF, 2023).

OCCURRENCE IN THE ST. VINCENT SURVEY: Recorded from three stations 13, 17, 22 in the St. Vincent survey. Five specimens were examined.

DESCRIPTION: A small species. Specimens of 6-20 mm CW were recorded in the survey. Maximum CW in males of 27 mm and females of 23.5 mm have been reported (Abele, 1992). Carapace is nearly square, with the length and breadth almost equal (Figure 66). The chelipeds are near equal in size and shape, and larger in males than females. The walking legs are long and flattened. Prominent eyes. The carapace is a mottled dark brown in colour. The fingers of the chelipeds are orange (Abele, 1992; Chance and Hobbs, 1969) (Figure 67).

RANGE: – The Antilles from Cuba to Trinidad (GBIF, 2023).

Figure 66. Dorsal view, *Armases roberti*.

Figure 67. Anterior view, *Armases roberti*, showing orange fingers of chelipeds.

HABITAT: – Recorded from 2 semi-estuarine pools and 1 rivulet station in the St. Vincent survey. The highest elevation at which the species was found was 8 m and within tens of metres from the sea. Numerous at the stations where it occurred. Semi-terrestrial, often see on the bank retreating into the river when disturbed. The locations where this species was occured were smaller streams (Chance and Hobbs, 1969). In St. Vincent, this species was found only in the lower reaches. In contrast, Chance and Hobbs (1969) observed it at 300 m elevation in Dominica. This species is capable of climbing: Chance and Hobbs (1969) observed it climbing a vertical surface on a bridge, and Von Hagen (1977) observed it climbing up bamboo.

FEEDING AND DIET: Analysis of stomach contents of *Armases roberti* from Trinidad indicate that plant material (algae and angiosperm) comprised most of the diet; detritus and insect material were also found (Von Hagen, 1977).

LIFE CYCLE AND REPRODUCTION: No females with eggs were found in the St. Vincent survey. Chance and Hobbs (1969) recorded berried females from freshwater in Dominica. Laboratory studies have shown that after hatching in freshwater, the first zoeal larval stage survives for only 2 days in a freshwater environment with optimal zoeal larval development taking place at a salinity of $25^0/_{00}$ (Diesel and Schuh, 1998, cited in Anger *et al.*, 2006). The final megalops larval stage survives in freshwater if acclimatised to progressively decreasing salinities. The development of megalops larvae into juvenile crabs is stimulated by scent cues produced by adults of the species (Anger *et al.*, 2006).

CONSERVATION STATUS (IUCN): Not assessed (IUCN, 2024).

IMPORTANCE TO FISHERIES: Not targeted by river fishermen in St. Vincent.

Other Freshwater Taxa Observed During the Survey

These are noted here for completeness of the survey record.

Phylum: Mollusca

Three species of Gastropod Molluscs: *Nereina punctulata* (Figure 68), *Ferrissia irrorata* (Figure 69), and *Melanoides tuberculata* (Figure 70) were observed during the survey. Table 7 provides further details.

Phylum: Chordata
Class: Amphibia
Family: Bufonidae

Larvae of the cane toad *Rhinella marina* were recorded from several locations during the survey. Table 8 provides further details.

Table 7. An inventory of mollusc species identified during the survey.

Scientific Name	Common Name	Status	Occurrence In St. Vincent	Habitat	Diet	Range	Previous Records from St. Vincent	IUCN Status
Nereina punctulata	River Whelk (vernacular in St. Vincent)	Native	Locally frequent	Foothill Torrent. Fast flowing clear water, stony substrate.	Algal film on stones.[1]	Caribbean, Central America, Northern South America[2]	Harrison and Rankin 1976	Not assessed
Ferrissia irrorata	Freshwater Limpet	Native	Locally frequent	Foothill Torrent. Fast flowing clear water, stony substrate.	Algal film on stones[3]	Southern US, Caribbean, Northern South America[2]	First described by Guilding from a specimen from St. Vincent in 1828[2]	Not assessed
Melanoides tuberculata	Red-rimmed Melania	Introduced Since 1976 Not recorded by Harrison &Rankin(1976)	Widespread and locally very abundant	Most common in semi-estuarine pools, also in foothill and mountain torrents.	Microalgae, detritus, aquatic plants[4]	Original range Africa (not West) and South Asia. Now global in tropical and sub-tropical regions[5]	A specimen from St. Vincent is lodged at the Carnegie Museum of Natural History[2]	Least concern[5]

References: [1] Pryon & Covich (2003), [2] GBIF Secretariat, [3] Museums Victoria Staff (2010), [4] Smithsonian Evnironmental Research Centre (2012), [5] Albrecht et al. (2018)

Table 8. An inventory of amphibian species identified during the survey.

Scientific Name	Life Stage	Common Name	Status	Occurrence In St. Vincent	Habitat	Diet	Range	Previous Records from St. Vincent	IUCN Status
Rhinella marina	Tadpole	Crapeau (vernacular in St. Vincent) Cane Toad	Introduced	Semi-estuarine pools and foothill torrents. Locally common.	Low flow areas.	Algae and aquatic plants[1]	Native range Northern South America, Trinidad[2]	IUCN SSC Amphibian Specialist Group[2]	Least concern[2]

References: [1] Aquarium of the Pacific web page, [2] IUCN SSC Amphibian Specialist Group (2023).

Figure 68. *Nereina punctulata*. (Photo S. Hornsey)

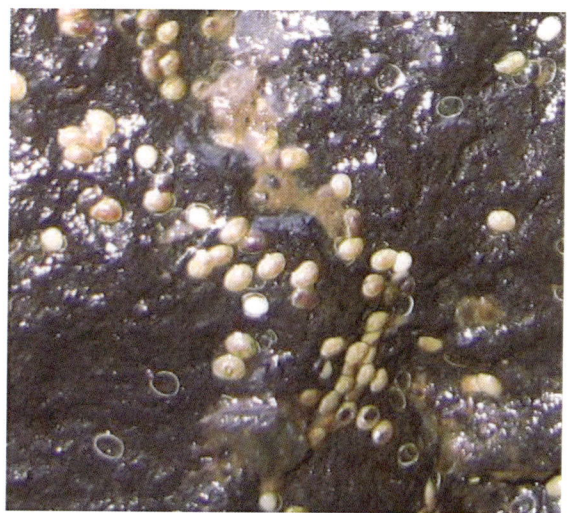

Figure 69. *Ferrissia irrorata*.

Figure 70. *Melanoides tuberculata*.

The Freshwater Fishery of St. Vincent

For most participants interviewed, river fishing provides a small part of their overall income under normal circumstances. However, the possession of fishing skills affords fishers and their families' greater economic resilience and food security during times of challenge. River fishermen take pride in their knowledge of the river and the species they target and many manufacture their own fishing gear. River fishing activity peaks during the season of Lent; though the religious obligation to fast from meat during this period has lapsed, the tradition of river fishing in this season remains. The findings of the survey of river fishermen are summarised in Table 9.

Table 9. Summary of the findings of the survey of river fishers.

QUESTIONS DIRECTED TO RIVER FISHERMEN	SUMMARY OF RESPONSES
Number of Fishers questioned	8
Gender	All male
Age of Fishermen	33-64 years, average 48 years
Do you catch fish/crayfish to sell?	Yes 3/8, Sometimes 5/8
Do you catch fish/crayfish for personal consumption?	Yes 7/8, Sometimes 1/8
How often do you eat river fish/crayfish	Frequently 1/8, Sometimes 4/8, Not often 3/8
Do you catch crayfish to use for bait?	Yes 1/8, No 7/8. catching bait was the primary reason for river fishing for the fisherman who answered "Yes".
Price for Fish.	$10-$12 for big fish, Macack $5/lb, price negotiable
Fish Species Sold.	Mullet 3/8, Grouper 3/8, Crocro 3/8, Macack 2/8, Eel 1/8
Price For River Lobster	$12-$25/lb, modal value $15/lb
Price For Crayfish	$10-$15/lb, modal value $10/lb
Is sale of river fish important income for you?	Big 1/8, Significant, 1/8, Small 5/8, None 1/8
Is sale of crayfish/lobster important income for you?	Big 1/8, Significant, 1/8, Small 6/8
Is the number of persons fishing in the river increasing or decreasing?	Increasing 3/8, Decreasing 5/8
Are species no longer present in the river?	Macfie. Suckstone decreasing.
Are river fish and crayfish as plentiful as before?	Yes 1/8, No 5/8
Factors that negatively impact catches by river fishermen..	- Poisoning 4/8 – some reduction in this observed by fishermen - Poor water quality prevents use of fishing with a face mask - Reduced flow in rivers - Agricultural chemical impacting water quality - River engineering that remover cover for lobsters and fish - Reduction in number of lobsters due to over fishing (Colonaire) - No regulation to control exploitation of river lobsters i.e. minimum size, ban on capture of berried females.

Patterns of Biodiversity

River Type

Person's Chi-squared tests were applied to investigate the association between the frequency of occurrence of fish species and crustacean species and river type recorded at survey stations (see Table 1 for river type classifications).

Table 10. Results of χ^2 Tests to investigate the association between frequency of occurrence of fish and decapod crustacean species and river type.

Taxa	River Types	χ^2	d.f.	p-value	
Fish	Major River Minor River	10.563	18	0.912	P>0.05 no significant difference
Decapod Crustaceans	Major river Minor River Stream	22.494	18	0.2108	P>0.05 no significant difference

There was insufficient data to include the river type category "stream" when examining the distribution of fish according to river type.

River types were classified by Harrison and Rankin (1976a) according to their height of origin above sea level. However they also tend to differ in size (volume, depth and width) with major rivers being the largest, followed by minor rivers and streams in that order. Results the Chi-squared test suggest that the differences between river types were not significant in determining fish and decapod distributions in the rivers in the study (Table 10).

Habitat Type

Person's Chi-squared tests were applied to investigate the association between the frequency of occurrence of fish species and crustacean species and habitat type recorded at survey stations (see Table 2 for habitat type classifications).

Table 11. The results of χ^2 Tests to investigate the association between frequency of occurrence of fish and decapod crustacean species and habitat type.

Taxa	Habitat Type	χ^2	d.f.	p-value	
Fish	Semi-estuarine Foothill Torrent Mountain Torrent	102.8	54	0.00007	P<0.05 significant difference
Decapod Crustaceans	Semi-estuarine Foothill Torrent Mountain Torrent	52.215	27	0.003284	P<0.05 significant difference

The results of the Chi-squared tests in Table 11 suggest that there was an association between the habitat type and the distributions of both fish and decapod crustaceans in the survey. The observed variation in the frequencies of occurrence of fish and decapod crustacean species with habitat type is illustrated in Figures 71 and 72. In summary, Figures 73 and 74 show sketches of the main habitat types, and provide associated occurrence/ distribution listings of fish and decapod species, as recorded by the present survey.

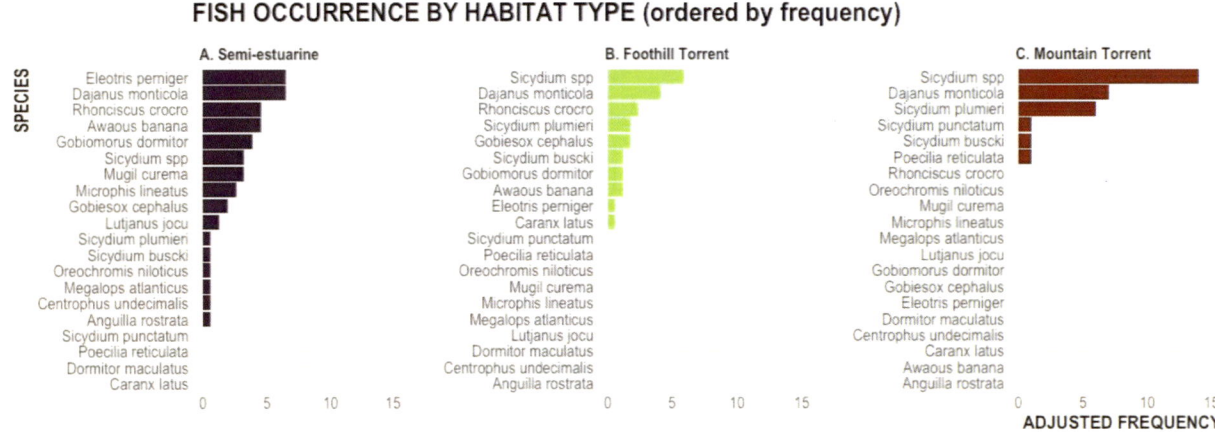

Figure 71. Trends in fish species occurrence in three major habitats. (Trends were adjusted for unequal sample sizes.)

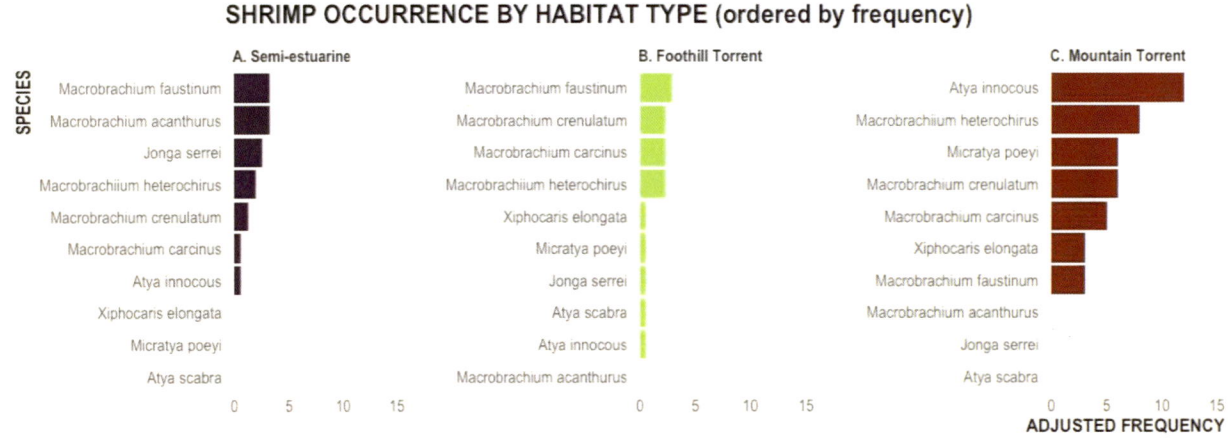

Figure 72. Trends in shrimp species occurrence in three major habits. **Trends were adjusted for unequal sample sizes.**

Semi-estuarine Pool

Sixteen fish species were recorded in the semi-estuarine pool habitat (Table 4, Figure 73). Several species, most commonly found in this habitat, were associated with mats of floating vegetation and muddy substrates which are only found in the low flow, occasionally brackish environment of the semi-estuarine pool. These species included *Microphis lineatus, Eleotris perniger* and *Gobiomorus dormitor.*
Several euryhaline, but predominantly marine species utilised the fresh or slightly brackish water found in this habitat. These included *Centropomus undecimalis, Lutjanus jocu, Megalops atlanticus, Mugil curema* and *Caranx latus.* Most individuals of this group captured in the survey were juveniles. These may enter the river to escape predators in the ocean or take advantage of an abundant food source e.g. post-larval fish and shrimp.
Nine species of decapod crustacean were recorded from the semi-estuarine pool (Tables 5 and 6, Figure 74). Two brackish water species, *Macrobrachium acanthurus* and *Callinectes sapidus*, were restricted to this habitat. *Jonga serrei* was most common in this habitat and was associated with emergent vegetation in low flow areas. Numerous juvenile *Macrobrachium* were found amongst emergent vegetation but were not identified to species.

Foothill Torrent

Nine species of fish were recorded from foothill torrent habitat (Figure 73). Several species, found in the semi-estuarine pool, were also present but occurred less frequently in foothill torrent stations. These included *Gobiomorus dormitor, Eleotris perniger, Awaous banana, Rhonciscus crocro* and *Gobiesox cephalus.* Adult *Sicydium* gobies which were less common in the semi-estuarine pool became more frequent over the stony substrate of the foothill torrent.
Nine species of decapod crustacean were recorded at foothill torrent stations (Figure 74). The only species exclusively recorded from a foothill torrent was *Atya scabra*, recorded at only one location. The species composition of the foothill torrent contains representatives of species more frequently found in the semi-estuarine pool and mountain torrent habitats.

Mountain Torrent

Five species of fish were recorded at mountain torrent stations (Figure 73). The dominant fish species of the mountain torrent were the *Sicydium* gobies, three species of the genus being recorded in this habitat. Fish biodiversity decreased with increasing elevation and distance from the sea. This may be partially the result of increasing probability of fish meeting a barrier to migration, a waterfall or a weir/dam, as they migrate up the river. In studies of fish distribution in Puerto Rico, Cooney and Kwak (2013) found that barriers of only 2 m restrict non goby migration and were prevented by barriers of 4 m. In contrast, *Sicydium* gobies, which are able to ascend waterfalls with the aid of the pelvic sucking disk, are only excluded by barriers greater than 32 m in height.
Eight species of decapod crustaceans were recorded at mountaintorrent stations (Figure 74). The crab *Guinotia dentata* was recorded only from this habitat. Six species of shrimp were most frequently recorded in mountain torrent habitats: *Xiphocaris elongata, Micratya poeyi, Atya innocous, Macrobrachium carcinus, Macrobrachium heterochirus* and *Macrobrachium crenulatum*. *Atya innocous,* in particular, can reach very high densities in mountain torrents (Figure 72). The increased frequency of occurrence of shrimp species in mountain torrent stations may be due to the absence of several predatory fish species e.g. *Gobiomorus dormitor, Eleotris perniger* and *Rhoncicus crocro* in this habitat type.

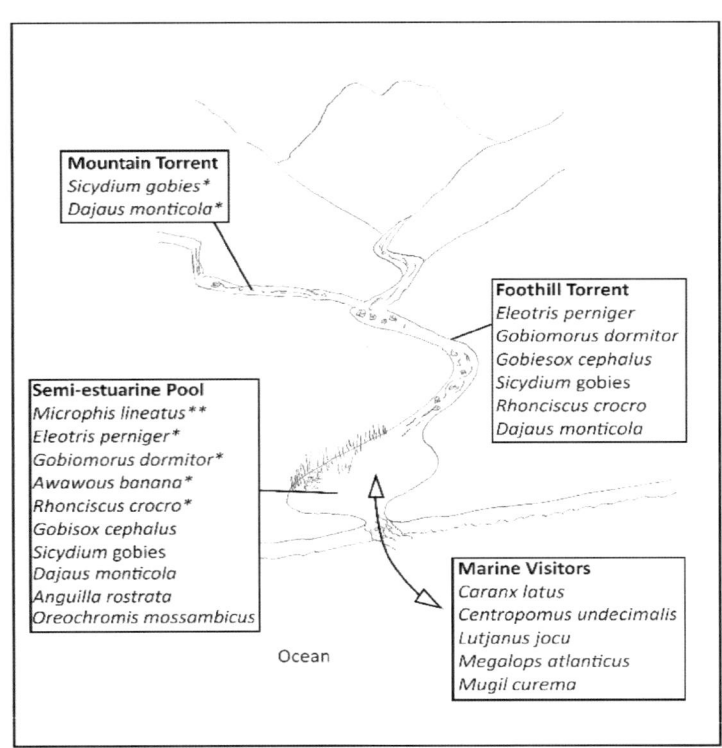

Figure 73. Fish species occurrence, according to location within the river system. (Key: ** confined to habitat, *most commonly occurring in habitat.)

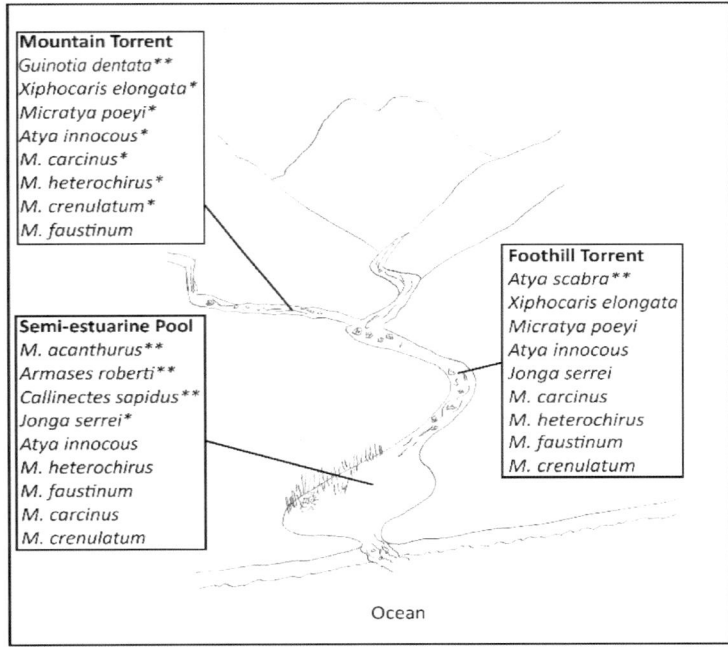

Figure 74. Decapod crustacean occurrence, according to location within the river system. (Key: ** confined to habitat, *most commonly occurring in habitat.)

The semi-estuarine pool was the most biodiverse, yet geographically restricted, habitat in the survey with 27 species of adult fish and crustaceans found there. This is not surprising as all fish and decapod crustacean species found in the river, with the exception of the crab *Guinotia dentata* and the fish *Poecillia reticulata,* are diadromous. The larvae of all diadromous species must pass through semi-estuarine pool on their migration to the sea and as post-larvae on their return to the river from the sea.

Feeding Relationships

Figure 75 shows a food web of river species from a stream in Guadeloupe, based on carbon isotope analysis of the food sources (Coat *et al.* 2009). The species in Figure 75 also occur in St. Vincent, with the exception of the apple snail, *Pomacea glauca*. The basal food sources and trophic organisation are likely to be similar in Vincentian rivers.

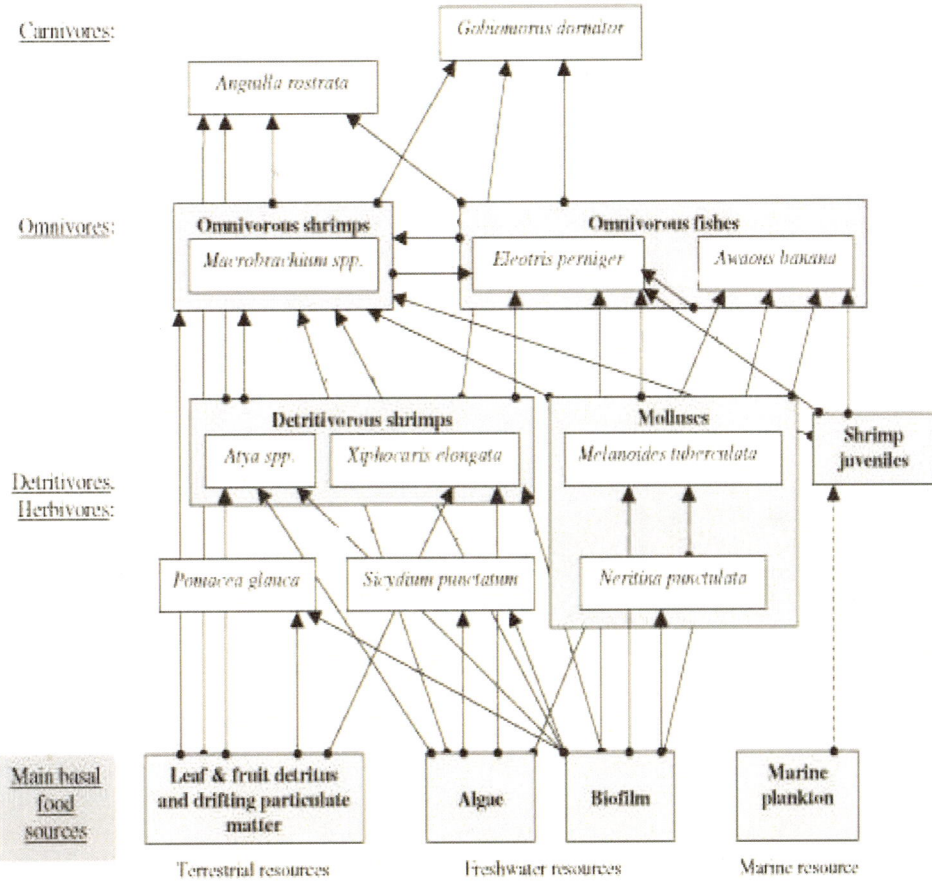

Figure 75. The food web of a Caribbean Stream, Grande-Anse, Guadeloupe. {Source: Coat *et al*. (2009) - The grey areas show similar carbon isotope signatures and represent the dominant food sources.}

The Freshwater and Brackish Water Fish and Decapod Diversity of St. Vincent Compared to Other Islands in the Ecoregion.

Abell *et al*. (2008) assigned the freshwater ecosystems of the Windward and Leeward Islands to a single ecoregion. The authors defined an ecoregion as a "large area encompassing one or more freshwater systems with distinct assemblages of natural freshwater communities and species". A comparison between the freshwater fauna recorded in the St. Vincent survey and the fauna of better studied islands within the Windward and Leeward Islands Ecoregion can be made.

The freshwater fish fauna of St. Vincent is very similar to the Eastern Caribbean-island of Guadeloupe. Guadeloupe shares 12 of 13 freshwater fish species recorded in the St. Vincent survey (Froese and Pauly, 2024; GBIF, 2023).

Species recorded in Guadeloupe but not in the present survey of St. Vincent include: the fat sleeper *Dormitator maculatus* (Figure 76), the large-scaled spinycheek sleeper, *Eleotris amblyopsis*, and mangrove rivulus, *Kryptolebias marmoratus.*

Personal observations of the fat sleeper were made at 3 locations in St. Vincent in 2007, from semi-estuarine pool habitats. Two of these locations, stations 22 and 26 were revisited in the 2023 survey, but no fat sleepers were found. Fishermen who were interviewed, indicated that they knew the fat sleeper by the local name 'macfi' and reported that they had not seen it for some time. The present status of this species in St. Vincent is unresolved.

A further study of a larger sample of Eleotridae from St. Vincent may reveal the presence of *E. amblyopsis*. A search of the limited mangrove habitat at Brighton produced no record of the mangrove rivulus for St. Vincent.

Figure 76. *Dormitator maculatus*, caught in the semi-estuarine pool of the Buccament River, 2007.

The freshwater and brackish water decapod crustacean fauna of the Eastern Caribbean-island of Dominica was thoroughly described by Chance and Hobbs (1969), and it is near identical to that found in the St. Vincent survey. Two relatively rare species were recorded in in Dominica but not in St. Vincent: the crab, *Callinectes bocourti*, and the shrimp, *Potimirim glabra*. Further sampling of the semi-estuarine pool for *Callinectes bocourti* and high headwater streams for *Potimirim glabra* in St. Vincent is likely to yield these species.

> **SUGGESTED CONSERVATION RESPONSE:**
> - Further surveys in St. Vincent to: ascertain if *Dormitator maculatus* is still extant; record any "rare" species missed in the survey; and, record any new invasive species that may arise. Future surveys could employ environmental DNA techniques to determine the species present. This methodology involves the identification of species by comparing the various DNA found in a sample of river water with previously studied DNA from species lodged in DNA libraries – metabarcoding.

An Overview of the IUCN Conservation Status of Species Recorded in the St. Vincent Survey

Table 12. Summary of the IUCN global conservation status of the species recorded in the St. Vincent Survey.

ICUN Status	Number of Fish Species	Number of Shrimp Species	Number of Crab Species	Total
Endangered	1	0	0	1
Vulnerable	1	0	0	1
Near Threatened	0	0	0	0
Least Concern	11	10	1	22
Data Deficient	4	0	0	4
Not Evaluated	1	0	2	3

International Union for Conservation of Nature (IUCN) Red List categorises species according to global risk of extinction based on population trend and size and size of geographical range. Two globally threatened species were recorded in the survey: the endangered American eel, *Anguilla rostrata*, and the vulnerable tarpon, *Megalops atlanticus*. Details regarding the conservation status of these species were previously discussed.

The majority of species occurring in the survey were categorised as 'of least concern' with regard to the threat of global extinction. Many of the species found in the survey in this group have large geographical ranges and populations are thought to be stable. Although not assessed as globally threatened, some species classified by the IUCN as 'of least concern' are locally threatened and have been awarded local conservation status. Examples included: the river lobster, *Macrobrachium carcinus*, which is over exploited in Brazil and is on the Brazilian Red List of threated species, the opossum pipefish, *Microphis lineatus*, is a species of concern in Florida due to its restricted and threatened habitat there.

Seven species (23%) recorded in the St. Vincent survey are categorised as 'Data Deficent' (i.e. data inadequate to determine threat category) or 'Not Evaluated'. Research is required to clarify the global and local conservation status of these species. In this regard, a species recorded in the survey, the riverine clingfish, *Gobisox cephalus*, is categorised as 'Data Deficient' by the IUCN River fishermen reported a local decline in numbers of this species. The IUCN (2012) manual on Red List

Categories and Criteria advises a cautious approach, and states clearly that species that are classified as 'Not Evaluated' or 'Data Deficient', "should not be treated as if they were non-threatened".

> SUGGESTED CONSERVATION RESPONSE:
> - Research is required to clarify the local conservation status of the fish classified as 'Not Evaluated' or 'Data Deficient' by the IUCN e.g. the riverine clingfish.
> - The IUCN Red List reports the global status of species. Local surveys are required to ascertain the local conservation status of species e.g. the previously recorded fat sleeper classified as 'of least concern' by the IUCN, but not found in the present survey.

Why No Endemic Freshwater Fish from St. Vincent?

The Caribbean is often described as a freshwater biodiversity hot spot, with 188 known native fish species and 60 (32%) of these being endemic to a single island (Phillip, 2017). Freshwater fish diversity is not uniformly distributed throughout the region. The majority of endemic freshwater fish species are found in Cuba and Hispaniola; a lesser number is found in the Bahamas, Jamaica and Trinidad and very few in the Lesser Antilles.

The distribution of fish families between islands separated by the ocean is dependent on the physiological ability of fish in that family to tolerate salt water and the geological history of the island. New species, island endemics, arise when a group within the species is separated and develops its own characteristics. Mayers (1949) classified freshwater fish into three groups according to their physiological ability to tolerate salt water. Primary (true) freshwater fish have very limited tolerance to brackish water. Dispersal across the ocean is impossible for this group. Secondary freshwater fish are largely confined to freshwater but can tolerate limited salinity. Limited dispersal across the ocean is possible for this group. Peripheral freshwater fish are members of predominantly marine families that reside, for most of their lives, in freshwater but are tolerant of salt water. Trinidad and the Greater Antilles are not true oceanic islands, and were once connected to North and South America. Over geological time, these islands were separated from the Americas by continental drift and sea level rise. Caribbean fish species in the primary division of freshwater fish (55 species) are found in the Greater Antilles and Trinidad because the sea represented an insurmountable barrier between the ancestral and island forms.

The majority of Caribbean freshwater fish species belong to the Secondary Division of freshwater fish. There are 104 species of secondary freshwater fish, from 9 families, in the Caribbean islands including: Synbranchidae (swamp eels) Chichillidae, Rivulidae (killifish), Poeciliidae, Fundulidae (topminnows), Cyprinodontidae (pupfish). Fish in the secondary division, though usually confined to freshwater, can survive short passages through salt water. The distances between Florida and Cuba, between the Yucatan peninsula and Cuba, and between Venezuela and Trinidad are relatively short. Unusual circumstances, for example, fish rafting across the ocean in mats of vegetation after floods may have carried some secondary freshwater species to and between the islands. Some species of Secondary freshwater fish have reproductive characteristics that increase the probability of the development of a new population as the result of chance dispersal. An example is the mangrove killifish *Kryptolebias marmoratus* which is widespread and is a self-fertilising hermaphrodite – only one individual is required to begin a new population. Natural selection operates on the new isolated population to select characteristics which increase the chance of survival in the new habitat. Over time, speciation occurs, resulting in island endemics.

Members of the peripheral division of freshwater fish are found in all Caribbean islands. There are 29 species of peripheral freshwater fish recorded in the region (Phillip, 2017). The Lesser Antilles are true oceanic islands and have never been connected to the mainland of the Americas, and have therefore been inaccessible to primary freshwater fish. Peripheral freshwater fish compose nearly all the fish fauna of the Lesser Antilles. Periferal freshwater fish families that occur in the region include: Anguillidae (freshwater eels), Eleotridae (sleepers), Gobiesocidae (clingfishes), Gobiidae (gobies), Mugilidae (mullets), and Syngnathidae (pipefishes). All fish in these families have a diadromous life cycle involving migration of larvae/post larvae from the sea into the river. Mixing of larvae originating from different rivers takes place at sea, and genetic studies suggest that returning larvae/post larvae do not have an affiliation to the river in which they were spawned (Cook *et al.*, 2009). The genetic separation required for new species to arise is unlikely to occur in Caribbean peripheral freshwater fish species, and is the reason for the lack of endemic freshwater fish in the Lesser Antilles.

Threats to Freshwater Biodiversity in St. Vincent

The biodiversity of the rivers of St. Vincent is under threat from natural and anthropogenic sources. Anthropogenic threats increase with population growth and development and the subsequent increased demand for water, energy, and urbanisation.

Volcanic Eruption

The impact of the April 2021 eruption on rivers with drainages on the slopes of Soufriere was varied. Four affected rivers were sampled in the survey.
The Fancy River was moderately impacted by ash, more so in the lower reaches. The area sampled (station 1) was a mountain torrent. A few small *Atya innocous, Micratya poeyi* and *Sicydium* gobies were found, suggesting the river had begun to recover.
The Kramaku River was relatively less impacted by ash with only some ashy deposits in pools. The station sampled (station 2) was a mountain torrent. Several shrimp species were found: *Macrobrachium carcinus, Macrobrachium heterochirus*, and *Micratya poeyi* were recorded; *Atya innocuous* was abundant. *Sicydium plumieri* was also recorded. Though under the volcano, this river escaped major impact and benefited from a moratorium on river fishing, applied to rivers impacted by the 2021 eruption and which was still in place at the time of the survey.
The Rabacca River was significantly impacted by the 2021 eruption. Pyroclastic flows and lahars flowed down the river destroying all life. Previous to the 2021 eruption, a brief survey of fish and shrimp was done in 2016 as part of an environmental impact assessment for the planned geothermal project on the bank of the Rabacca River (Environmental Resource Management 2016). Five species of shrimp were found: *Macrobrachium carcinus, Macrobrachium heterochirus, Macrobrachium crenulatum, Macrobrachium faustinum;* and, two fish species *Sicydium plumieri, Gobiesox sp.*. This is a fair biodiversity despite the lower reaches of the Rabacca River being a bourne or "dry river" in all but heavy rain restricting access to the sea. In the present 2023 survey, (Station 3), the riverbed was filled with clean boulders. Ash and lahar deposits on the valley floor were incised by the river channel which was bordered by a lahar terrace. Dense forest remained beside the river; although the river corridor had been widened, the canopy did not reach the river. No fish or shrimp were found at this site in 2023. The extent of the dry section of the Rabacca River post-eruption was increased and there was a significant waterfall below the sample station. These factors may have hindered recolonization from the sea.

The Wallibou River (station 40) was impacted by pyroclastic flows and lahars during and after the eruption in April 2021. Pyroclastic flows filled the riverbed with ash, creating a dry river (Figure 77). These were followed by lahars after which the river ran over the surface again in many braided channels (Figure 78). At first the riverbed was unstable, small rocks constantly rolled downstream and the water carried a heavy load of suspended sediment, which was visible as a large plume of discoloured water out to sea. By the sampling date in March 2023, the river had eroded downwards through the ash deposits (Figure 79) and was confined to one main and two lesser channels. By this time, the riverbed had become more stable and was composed of boulders and cobble. On visiting the same location in 2006 (a pre-eruption year), the following species were observed: fish species - *Dajaus monticola, Gobiesox cephalus, Awaous banana* and adult and juvenile *Sicydium;* shrimp species - *Macrobrachium heterochirus, Macrobrachium crenulatum* and juvenile *Xiphocaris elongata.* In March 2023, 22 months after the 2021 eruption, *Dajaus monticola* were frequently found and *Rhonciscus crocro* occasionally occurred, while juvenile *Macrobrachium* and *Sicydium* gobies were rare. Some stones in the riverbed were covered in a film of green algae. Although the river was not yet completely stable, the presence of mountain mullet, crocro and juvenile macack indicate partial recovery. It is not clear if the mountain mullet and crocro were resident in the river or making an opportunistic foray from the sea. It is interesting to note that large runs of 'tritri' into the Wallibou River occurred post eruption despite the river system having an unstable bed and being unable to support juvenile macack at that time.

It appears that post eruption recovery of the aquatic ecosystem has begun in rivers that remain flowing above ground. Studies of fluvial recovery of rivers following an eruption of the Mt. Pinatubo volcano by Gran and Montgomery (2005) indicate that channel stability precedes aquatic ecological recovery. The St. Vincent survey took place in the dry season when flow was lowest. Further destabilisation of the riverbed may still occur due to lahars, erosion and landslides during periods of heavy rainfall in the wet season and these may set back biological recovery. The majority of fish and shrimps that inhabit Vincentian Rivers are amphidromous. The amphidromous life cycle will facilitate recovery as the post-larvae of these taxa are expected to recolonise the river from the sea.

Figure 77. Wallibou River on 13th April 2021 after a pyroclastic flow. (Photo, UWI Seismic)

Figure 78. Wallibou River December 2021.

Figure 79. Wallibou River, Station 40, March 2023.

Flow Modification

Water abstraction

Water abstraction from rivers, for hydroelectric generation and domestic water supply, changes the volume and timing of flow which, in turn, impact the availability of the river as a habitat and the physical and chemical nature of that habitat.

The Central Water and Sewage Authority (CWSA) operates 15 surface intakes, which supply 94% of the water supplied to consumers in St. Vincent. Every day, 27 million litres of water are abstracted from the rivers. In the dry season, demand for water exceeds supply in some catchments and seasonal rationing is required. This level extraction must reduce the flow in the rivers, especially in the dry season.

St. Vincent Electricity Services Limited (VINLEC) operates hydroelectric power plants in St. Vincent at: Richmond (1.1MW), South Rivers (0.9MW), and Cumberland (3.6MW) (VINLEC web page 2023). Water from the Richmond River is diverted through pipes to the generating station in an adjacent valley. On the day of sampling for the present survey, all water in the Richmond River had been diverted, leaving the riverbed dry for 2.5km and creating an artificial dry river below the intake (Figure 80). Sampling the flowing river above the intake (stations 38 and 39) produced only two shrimp species: less diversity than comparable mountain torrent stations. River fishermen from Spring Village reported reduced catches in the sections of the Cumberland River where flow is reduced by water abstraction. On sampling the Colonarie River, in the area of South Rivers Power Station, the river was observed to flow powerfully above the intake but was reduced to a series of pools with little water flowing between them below the intake. Large numbers of *Sicydium* gobies were concentrated within these pools. The survey took place in the dry season when naturally reduced flow was exacerbated by water abstraction.

Hydro power provides 18-20% of the annual electricity generated in SVG (Vinlec Web Page 2023). Electricity demand increased from 21.84MW in 2020 to 23MW in 2023, and is projected to continue to rise (St. Vincent Times, 20/1/24). Hydroelectric power is often perceived as a green source of energy as it is renewable and does not produce carbon emissions. Despite the challenge of increased demand for electricity, water abstraction for hydro generation should be managed to minimise ecological impacts.

Figure 80. The Richmond River below the intake of the hydro plant during the dry season.

> **SUGGESTED CONSERVATION RESONSE:**
> - Establish **environmental flow** – the quantity and timing of flow required to sustain the river ecosystem. The CWSA is charged with the conservation, control and apportionment of water to maintain the water supply for domestic, agricultural and industrial purposes under the CWSA Act (1992). The establishment of an agreed environmental flow would involve negotiation between the CWSA, others who abstract water (VINLEC, farmers), and agencies/ bodies responsible for conservation and management of biodiversity (Fisheries Division, Forestry Division, National Parks Authority, fisher folk). This negotiation should be informed by research. Special emphasis should be placed on rivers that support tritri and river lobster fisheries.
> - The design of any future hydroelectric plants should minimise impacts on the river ecosystem. Low headwater dams that impede migration of the larvae and juveniles of fish species e.g. the endangered American eel and *Sicydium* gobies. Water abstracted should be returned to the same river. Measures should be taken to exclude fish e.g. the endangered American eel from entering the turbines.
> - Reduce demand on the water supply system and the need to remove water from rivers by increasing rainwater harvesting. Demand for potable water is increasing as a result of urbanisation and the expansion of the tourism industry. Increased droughts are a predicted impact of climate change in the region. Similar issues also face Mexico City where demand for water exceeds supply. The authorities there have responded by incorporating rainwater harvesting into the city's constitution regulations. The new policy outlines technical and financial support for rainwater harvesting and mandates dual pipe systems in new buildings (Mares, 2024). Rainwater harvesting is already extensively practiced in the Grenadines, and hence technical expertise is already present in the State. Existing financial support mechanisms for rainwater harvesting e.g. the General Cooperative Credit Union's low-interest flexible loan for purchase of water tanks should be expanded.

River Engineering

Several instances of major alteration of the course and flow of rivers have occurred in St. Vincent. River engineering is often, but not exclusively, found in the lower reaches of the river. These works involve straightening and channelising the river. Examples include the works to prevent flooding at the Buccament Resort (Figure 81), the mouth of the Warrawarrow River in Arnos Vale and construction of a culvert to contain the Yambou River as it passes under the runway of Argyle International Airport. Channelising the rivers results in loss of back water habitat. Similarly, removal of boulders results in loss of cover for river lobster and "grouper".
Weirs and low headwater dams (Figure 82), which alter the natural flow of the river, are known to impede the migration of juvenile, diadromous species limiting their access to the river system (Cooney and Kwak, 2013).

Figure 81. Channel alteration made at the lower Buccament River in April 2022.

Figure 82. Hydroelectric dam on the Cumberland River at Spring Village.

Climate Change

The Regional Circulation Models developed by the Climate Studies Group of the University of the West Indies have been used to estimate the climate of the Windward Islands for the remainder of the 21st century. The models used low (RCP 2.6), medium (RCP 4.5) and high (RCP 8.5) greenhouse gas emissions projection scenarios (Van Meerbeek et al., 2021).

Extreme Rainfall
Models predict that the proportion of rainfall for extremely wet days will increase and that the annual number of heavy rain days will decrease over the 21st century. The extent of these trends increases with the level of emissions (Van Meerbeek et al., 2021). More intense periods of heavy rain will result in increased probability of flash floods.
Flood events potentially impact river ecology in several ways. Floods disrupt habitat by altering channels, pools and banks, and displacing organisms downstream. Floods also impact population survival by physically damaging organisms, influencing upstream migration and altering food webs. Covich et al. (1991) investigated the number and distribution of the shrimp, *Atya lanipse*, in a mountain steam in Puerto Rico before and after the passage of hurricane Hugo in September 1989. In the month following Hugo, numbers of *A. lanipse* were reduced by 50% in the headwaters and increased by 80% in midsections of the river, due to downstream displacement. In the following six months, highest ever numbers of *A. lanipse* were recorded from all sections. The authors suggest that this was due to the addition of decomposing forest leaves, a food source for these shrimp, to the river during the hurricane. In another study, Covich et al. (2006) recorded the numbers of *Macrobrachium* shrimp in the Quebrada Prieta, Puerto Rico, over a period of 15 years during which time storm events and droughts occurred. The *Macrobrachium* species in this study, *M. carcinus, M. heterochirus, M. faustinum* and *M. crenulatum*, also occur in St. Vincent. No change in numbers of *Macrobrachium* related to storm events was found.
These studies suggest that shrimp species have capacity to recover from and even benefit from flood events of moderate magnitude. The ecological impact of more intense flood events, like the St. Vincent Christmas Eve flood of 2013 a 1 in 100 year event in which 200-310 mm of rain fell in 2-3 hours, is less well known. The human impact of this flood was severe, 11 lives were lost and 291.4 million XCD in damage occurred (Gov. SVG, 2014) (Figure 83). All rivers were impacted. Ten years later, reports by river fishermen and the biodiversity recorded in the present survey suggest that the river fauna has recovered from this event. The ability of the largely diadromous fauna's larvae to recolonise from the sea affords the fauna resilience.

Figure 83. The Buccament River, Vermont, on 11th January 2014, showing erosion of the bank and scouring of the riverbed caused by the 2013 Christmas Eve Flood.

Drought

Meteorological drought is defined as a deficit in rainfall over a specified time. Hydrological drought occurs if the period of rainfall deficit extends long enough to impact streams and rivers. A short-term hydrological drought occurs after several weeks to 6 months of rainfall deficit. This duration of drought will impact river ecology. In order to ascertain if projected rainfall is in deficit, projected rainfall is compared to baseline information (1961-1990), based on historical climate data for the territory. The proportional anomaly between the baseline data and the projected rainfall over a specified time period is known as the Standard Precipitation Index (SPI). Models assuming moderate and high carbon emissions predict an increase in drought in the Windward Islands from 2030s. The moderate emissions model (RCP 4.5) predicts a SPI index of -0.6 for a 6 month data period and a SPI index of -1.4 (very dry) for a 12 month data period by the end of the century. The high emissions model (RCP 8.5) predicts a SPI index of -0.8 (moderately dry) for a 6 month data period and a SPI index of -1.8 (extremely dry) for a 12 month data period by the end of the century (Van Meerbeek *et al.*, 2021).
Studies indicate that droughts have a greater negative impact than floods on river ecology. Rainfall deficits can be prolonged, e.g. the 2014-2016 Caribbean drought (Van Meerbeek *et al.*, 2021). Drought reduces stream flow, dissolved oxygen, availability of habitat and connectivity within the stream. Water quality is reduced by concentration of contaminants and increase in algal growth. The impacts of droughts are exacerbated by water abstraction for hydro power and domestic supply. Covich *et al.* (2006) studied of the numbers of *Macrobrachium* shrimp in Quebrada Prieta, Puerto Rico, over a 15 year period. The lowest numbers of *Macrobrachium* shrimp were recorded during a year of drought. *Macrobrachium* species were absent from some parts of their former habitat for three years following the drought event. Sufficient flow is required to maintain connectivity within the stream, and also between the river and the ocean. The larvae of amphidromous species require sufficient flow to carry them down stream in a timely manner to the sea to limit the high mortality involved in this dangerous migration (Bell, 2009). Peak migration of *Sicydium* post-larvae, tritri, takes place between June and January (Engman, 2017). This period corresponds approximately to the rainy season. Sufficient flow is required for post larvae to migrate from the sea into the river and for juveniles to migrate further into the river system. Drought occurring in the peak post-larval migration period potentially impacts the tritri fishery.

Increased Temperature

Regional Circulation Models, run for low, medium and high carbon emission scenarios, predict an increase in air temperature in the Windward Islands. The frequency of hot days (>32°C) is predicted to increase eight-fold from baseline data and to be close to 100% in the 2040s. Heat waves, during which temperatures in the top 10% of the temperature range occur for at least 6 consecutive days, are expected be recorded for near to 300 days per annum by the 2030s (Van Meerbeek *et al.*, 2021). Increased air temperatures will result in increased river water temperatures. Increase in water temperature results in a decrease in the ability of oxygen to dissolve in it. An increase in river water temperature may result in an environment that is outside of the thermal tolerance of some river fauna. Tropical ectotherms (fish, shrimp, molluscs) live closely to their upper thermal tolerance limit (Nash *et al.*, 2021). The thermal tolerance limit is not known for many species in the Vincentian fauna. However, a study by Diaz *et al.* (2002) found the preferred water temperature of *Macrobrachium acanthurus* to be 29.9°C and the critical thermal maximum of 38°C. Water temperatures exceeding the preferred range may have nutritional and reproductive impacts on ectothermic species resulting in ecological change.

Pollution

Some informal observations regarding water quality were made during the survey. No point sources of pollution were seen. The colour of the river water was observed at each station. At 4/40 stations the water was described as grey in colour suggesting low water quality. Three of these stations were semi-estuarine pools with low flow (stations 17, 23, 30), two flowed through residential areas (stations 17, 23). The middle reaches (foothill torrents) are subject to increasing urbanisation, agricultural runoff (pesticides, fertilizer and effluent from pig farms). Poor water quality prevents the use of the diving mask when fishing in polluted areas. Public perception of poor water quality from some rivers prevents the sale of tritri caught in some locations.

> SUGGESTED CONSERVATION RESPONSE:
> - At present, the monitoring of water quality of potable and recreational water falls within the scope of the Environmental Mangement Department of the Ministry of Health, Wellness and the Environment. Expansion of water quality monitoring (physical, chemical and biological), to include monitoring of the health of the river as an ecosystem, is needed.
> - Increased resourcing for monitoring water quality is necessary.

Pesticide Runoff

St. Vincent was heavily involved in banana production between the 1950s and the 1980s, a crop known to require significant pesticide application. Banana cultivation was also important in Martinique. In Martinique, the organochloride pesticide, chlordecone, was used to control the banana root borer. Organochloride pesticides are now banned because they have been found to be carcinogenic. They are stable compounds and remain in the environment for many decades and bio-accumulate in the food chain. In Martinique, no consumption of freshwater fishery products from contaminated areas is permitted as unsafe levels of pesticide have been found in the flesh of river fish and crayfish (Multigner *et al.*, 2016). The mortality rate from prostate cancer in St. Vincent and the Grenadines ranks 6th in the world and is the 3rd most frequent cause of death (World Health Rankings - 2024). Organochloride pesticides have been banned for some time in SVG but data on their use in the early years is difficult to obtain. If organochloride pesticides were used in St. Vincent, they will still be present in the environment.

> SUGGESTED CONSERVATION RESPONSE:
> - Testing of the tissues of river fish, crayfish and tritri tissue for organochloride pesticides is urgently required to determine if these are safe for human consumption.

Invasive Species

Two freshwater fish species recorded in the survey are invasive, the Mozambique tilapia, *Oreochromis mossambicus*, and the guppy, *Poecelia reticulata*. These species have the potential to negatively impact the local ecology. Both reproduce rapidly, have a wide environmental tolerance, and have the potential to outcompete the native species for food.

O. mossambicus was also recognised as one of the world's 100 worst invasive species by the Invasive Species Specialist Group of the IUCN in 2014, as it has been widely introduced for aquaculture purposes. The most significant negative impacts of *O. mossambicus* as an invasive have been on populations of rare species with a restricted range e.g. the critically endangered Bahama pup fish, *Cyprinodon laciniatus* (Fofonoff *et al.*, 2018). *O. mossambicus* is believed to have been present in St. Vincent since the 1980s when it escaped from an experimental aquaculture facility in the Buccament Valley. The species appears to remain restricted in its distribution and was recorded from only one location in the survey possibly due to its requirement for a snady or muddy substrate for reproduction. The guppy or million fish was introduced in historical times, probably for biological control of mosquitos. The species is relatively rare in fast flowing rivers but widespread in drains, gutters and springs.

Introduced fish species comprise 15% of the freshwater fish occurring in St. Vincent. Other Caribbean islands have suffered greater impacts from invasive species. In Puerto Rico, invasive freshwater fish comprise 37 of 46 (80%) freshwater fish species reported (Rodriguez-Barreras *et al.* 2020). The majority of invasive freshwater fish species in Puerto Rico have been introduced through the aquarium pet trade. The problem of invasive freshwater fish is not as extreme in St. Vincent as the culture of aquarium fish keeping is not prevalent here.

Two additional freshwater invasive species were found in the survey. Tadpoles of the cane toad, *Rhinella marina*, were common in low flow areas. This species was introduced historically to control insect pests. Tadpoles are poisonous to most species and so do not provide a food source. The snail, *Melanoides tuberculata*, was introduced at some point after Harrison and Rankin's (1976) study, and it is now extremely numerous in some locations. Introduction was probably accidental. *Melanoides tuberculata* grazes algae, is eaten by fish and birds, and is an intermediate host for at least 37 parasite species (Fofonoff *et al.* 2018). The ecological impact of these species is not known.

> **SUGGESTED CONSERVATION RESPONSE:**
> - Continued vigilance is required by the Ministry of Agriculture, Forestry Fisheries and Rural Transformation regarding the importation of exotic pet species with the potential to become invasive in national freshwater habitats.

Exploitation by Fisheries

The Tritri Fishery
The tritri fishery, previously described, is the most significant freshwater fishery in St. Vincent. Anecdotal reports suggest that tritri catches are declining in St. Vincent. *Sicydium* post-larval fisheries are also reported to be in decline in Jamaica, Puerto Rico, and Dominica (Bell, 1999). Tritri fisheries are occasional and artisanal in nature, which makes the collection of data on the fishery difficult. The tritri fishery targets post-larvae. Mortality is naturally highest at this stage in the life cycle and the fish stock is best able to withstand fishing mortality at this point. Engman *et al.* (2021) estimated fishing mortality at 5.8 -7% of the post-larval run in Puerto Rico, and suggested that this level of exploitation was sustainable. Many factors, in addition to exploitation, influence the number of returning post-larvae. For example, habitat degradation can reduce the number of breeding adults in the river, larval survival, and the growth rate of the larvae at sea. The fishery in St. Vincent is impacted by the loss of traditional fishing sites due to coastal development, and by customer resistance to purchase of tritri from rivers with poor water quality. Research is required to quantify the status of the culturally and economically important tritri fishery in St. Vincent.

> **SUGGESTED CONSERVATION RESPONSE:**
> - Conduct research to collect data on the status of the resource (recruitment, growth, mortality) and carry out a scientific assessment of the *Sicydium* post-larval fishery.
> - Conduct research on the social and economic aspects of the fishery.
> - Use the fishery assessment and the socio-economic data and information to develop a sustainable management plan for the tritri fishery.
> - Seek partnership and funding with a suitable research institution for a PhD student to carry out the above.
> - Genetic studies are necessary to ascertain the extent to which the *Sicydium* stock or stocks are shared between islands. Regional management may be required.

The River Lobster Fishery

The river lobster, *Macrobrachium carcinus,* is the most highly valued product of the river, with the exception of tritri, and affords a price of $12-$25 per pound (median value - $15 XCD per pound Table 9). Some fishermen exploit this species on a semi-professional basis, and catch according to demand. Fishing pressure on river lobster is locally high. Reduced catches and sizes of lobsters caught are reported by fishermen from the Colonaire River, which is suggestive of over exploitation. At present, there is no fisheries legislation referring to this species in St. Vincent. Some fishermen, who were interviewed, support a minimum size limit and prohibition on the capture of berried females as measures to conserve the river lobster fishery.

> **SUGGESTED CONSERVATION RESPONSE:**
> - Consider the addition of river lobsters to the Schedule 3 (Partially Protected Species) of the Wildlife Protection Act (SVG Gov 1987) so that regulations could be put in place if required. Consideration should be given to the need for prohibition of the capture of undersized river lobsters and berried females, and banning of harmful fishing methods.
> - Hold stakeholder meetings with river fishers to ascertain their opinions regarding river lobster conservation.

The American Eel

The American eel is classified as an endangered species by the IUCN This species is targeted in the yellow and silver eel phase by five out of eight river fishermen interviewed in St. Vincent. Fishermen also report a decline in the numbers of this species. Internationally, juvenile eels (elvers) have been heavily exploited in Canada and Maine, USA. There is a very high demand for elvers to grow out purposes in Asian fish farms. In early 2024 the price for live elvers reached $5000 Canadian per kg. Only a regulated number of licence holders were previously allowed to fish. However high prices have resulted in a surge in poaching, violence on the fishing grounds and smuggling of elvers. In 2024, the Minister of Fisheries of Canada said "it is not possible to have a safe and sustainable elver fishery" and the fishery has been closed (Withers, Feb. 13 2024). Illegal elver fishing is now occurring in the Caribbean. In February 2024, the US Coast Guard apprehended two Dominicans who were attempting to smuggle 22 bags of live elvers out of Puerto Rico, where American eels are protected by law. The District Attorney of Puerto Rico, Stephen Muldrow, said it was "important for the government to combat these organised crimes as they pose a threat to the country's biodiversity" (Loop News, March 4th 2024).

> **SUGGESTED CONSERVATION RESPONSE:**
> - In view of the international classification of the American eel as an endangered species, consideration should be made regarding protection of this species in St. Vincent by adding it to the list of protected species in Schedule 2 of the Wildlife Protection Act (SVG Gov. 1987). This provision would make fishing for, being in possession of, and sale of the species illegal.
> - The fishing gear used in the survey did not effectively sample for the American eel. An electrofishing survey is required to ascertain data on the density and distribution of this endangered species in St. Vincent.
> - Educational outreach, aimed at increasing public awareness that the eel is an endangered species and of the threats faced by the eel and the freshwater environment in general, is required.

River Poisoning

Natural plant-based fish poisons was used historically in the Caribbean. Price (1966) quotes Brenton (1665), "The island Caribs use a variety of fish poisons both in fresh and salt water". Fishermen report that tobacco juice, pepper, cassava water and plants known as poison bush are used to catch crayfish. More powerful, industrially produced pesticides e.g. Carbaril (Sevin), Malathion, bleach and cement are also used. "The practice of the use of an explosive, poison or other noxious substance for killing, stunning, disabling, or catching fish" is prohibited In St. Vincent and the Grenadines under The Fisheries Act (1986), Gov. SVG Min. of Ag. Web Page The use of pesticides damages the environment by reducing abundance of fish and shrimp, reducing biodiversity and changing species composition. Effects on the human population include risk to health from contaminated fish and shrimp, loss of a source of food, loss of potential income from fishing (Betts et al., 2020). Four out of eight river fishermen surveyed identified fishing with poison as a reason for concern. Patrolling by Forestry Officers is a deterrent to poisoners as the process of collecting the catch after poisoning a river takes some time during which the offenders are at risk being apprehended or reported by the public. Two fishermen reported that the incidence of fishing with poison has declined due to increased public awareness and patrols by the Forestry Department.

The severity of environmental damage caused by a poisoning event and subsequent recovery are affected by many variables, including the type of poison used, the length of the reach impacted, and the flow at the time. Forestry Officers reported that a survey station on the Grand Sable River (station 5) was poisoned three weeks prior to sampling. Two species of fish and two species of shrimp, including juvenile river lobster were recorded, suggesting some recovery. A study by Greathouse et al. (2005) on the recovery of a Puerto Rican river, after a bleach poisoning event, suggests that the poisoned reach acts like a sink and is repopulated from the surrounding unaffected areas. It is possible that Station 5 was repopulated in this manner. Frequent poisoning would negatively impact recovery in this scenario.

> **SUGGESTED CONSERVATION RESPONSE:**
> - Continued patrolling by Forestry Division Enforcement Officers.
> - Public awareness activities to sensitise the public regarding the law concerning river poisoning, the possible health danger regarding consumption of poisoned fish and crayfish, and the damage caused to river ecology by this practice.

Traditional Fishing

Artisanal river fishing using traditional methods is unlikely to result in over exploitation of the majority of fish and crayfish species. Fishing effort is low, with the possible exception of river lobster in some rivers. It is likely that these fisheries would self-regulate – if target species became too small or presented too much effort to catch, fishermen would stop fishing until recovery occurred. River fishing has potential for development as an ecotourism product, which will add value to the natural heritage by providing employment and utilizing the traditional knowledge of river fishermen.

> **SUGGESTED CONSERVATION RESPONSE:**
> River fishing has often been viewed by decision makers as a fringe activity of little economic importance or cultural significance. Measures to increase representation by traditional river fishers, and public awareness of the value of traditional tritri and river fishing practices are required including –
> - Champions from among the river and tritri fishers to voice their needs and concerns are required. Participation by tritri and river fishers in the National Fisherfolk Organisation is a possible vehicle by which tritri and river fishers' interests could be represented.
> - Promotion of ecotourism tourism products which give visitors a traditional fishing experience e.g. fishing for crayfish with a basket in a mountain stream. An example of such a product in St. Vincent is posted at -
> https://www.viator.com/tours/Kingstown/River-Fishing-in-St-Vincent/d4322-10197P2
> This type of touism creates employment for river fishermen, adds sustainabe economic value to rivers and values traditional knowledge about river species and fishing methods.

A Habitat under Threat – The Semi-Estuarine Pool

The semi-estuarine pool is of unique ecological significance. It was the most biodiverse habitat in the survey. Fifteen species of fish and nine species of decapod crustaceans were recorded from this habitat. The opossum pipe fish and five brackish water/marine fish species were only recorded from this habitat. Two decapods, the blue crab and *Macrobrachium acanthurus* are restricted to the semi-estuarine pool. In addition, the semi-estuarine pool is the vital link that connects the river to the sea. The larvae of amphidromous taxa, the majority of fish, shrimp and molluscs, found in our rivers must pass through the semi-estuarine section of river on their way to the sea to develop and also on their return to the river as post-larvae or juveniles. Degradation of this habitat potentially negatively impacts the ecology of the entire river.

The semi-estuarine pool habitat is particularly vulnerable to anthropogenic threats and is the most threatened river habitat in St. Vincent due to its limited occurrence and restricted area. Sea front land is increasingly sought after for development. Development around the river mouth often results in channel alteration and canalisation. Pollution and reduction in water quality originating from higher sections of the river impacts the semi-estuarine pool. Coat *et al*. (2011) observed strong bioaccumulation of organochloride pollutants in juvenile shrimp and fish as they entered the river.

> **SUGGESTED CONSERVATION RESPONSE:**
> - Consider affording protected area status to river mouths where tritri fisheries operate (Wallibou, Petit Bordel, Cumberland, Bucament, Colonaire) under the Fisheries Act or the National Parks Act.

The Institutional and Legal Mechanisms for the Conservation of Freshwater Biodiversity in St. Vincent and the Grenadines

No single body has sole responsibility for the management of biodiversity in St. Vincent and the Grenadines. Aspects of the use of freshwater resources and preservation of wildlife therein are covered under several Acts of Government and by multiple Departments of Government.

The Ministry of Health, Wellness and the Environment is charged with the delivery of appropriate environmental health practices and environmental stewardship. The Environmental Engineering Unit is focused on monitoring environmental parameters including recreational and potable water quality and effluent discharge. The Conservation and Sustainable Development Unit co-ordinates activities and reporting regarding all environmental conventions, agreements and protocols of which SVG is a signatory e.g. The UN Convention on Biological Diversity. Other activities within the remit of this unit include: reducing the effects of land degradation, adaptation to climate change, sustainable use of biological resources and raising awareness of environmental issues (Ministry of Health Web Page, 2024).

The Economic Planning Unit of The Ministry of Finance, Economic Planning and Information Technology is responsible for planning the sustainable economic development of St. Vincent and the Grenadines including setting development goals and sourcing funding to support these (Ministry of Finance … web page, 2024).

The CWSA Act, 1992, affords the Central Water and Sewage Authority ultimate control of freshwaters in St. Vincent and the Grenadines. Section 12 gives the CWSA "the control of such water for the public benefit" in the first instance for provision of water for domestic, agricultural and commercial purposes but also including fishing and the preservation of flora and fauna.

The Forestry Department of the Ministry of Agriculture, Forestry, Fisheries and Rural Transformation includes a Forestry Law and Compliance Unit, a Wildlife Unit and an Education Unit. The greatest capacity for the conservation of river biodiversity resides within the Forestry Department. The activities of the Forestry Department are governed by two Acts –

1. The Forest Resource Conservation Act, 1992. The title of the Act refers to "the conservation, management and proper use of the forests and watersheds". The Act stipulates that the Forestry Department of the Ministry of Agriculture, Forestry Fisheries and Rural Transformation produce a periodic conservation plan to include water resources. This plan involves input from the CWSA and VINLEC, among others, before publication. The focus of the Act is the protection and conservation of the water supply as an essential human resource. The conservation of the watershed for this purpose also maintains the river as a biological habitat. Section 5 (1) (h) makes reference to "maintenance of biological diversity" as a function of the Director of Forestry.

2. The Wildlife Protection Act, 1987, stipulates legislation to protect wildlife. "Fishes, their fry and eggs" and "crustaceans" are classified as wildlife under section 2 of the Act. The Act refers to hunting regulations, regulations pertaining to human activities in wildlife reserves, lists partially protected and protected species, and describes powers of enforcement. No freshwater species are currently protected under the Act.

The National Parks Act, 2002, legislates for the establishment of the National Parks, Rivers and Beaches Authority. Section 7 (1) states that the Authority "shall have power and control over all rivers, streams, springs, swamps, waterfalls, waterpools and beaches in the State". Section 7 (2) outlines the functions of the Authority which include paragraph (b) "promote of conservation", (f) "ensure protection of species and habitats, especially species which are threatened, rare, endemic and commercial species and representative habitats", (g) "undertake the replenishment or rehabilitation of depleted fish and invertebrate stocks". The Authority falls within the Ministry of Tourism, Civil Aviation, Sustainable Development and Culture and its resources are largely focused on the management of 18 recreation/tourist sites across the State. The staff of the Authority engage in educational outreach to promote conservation awareness.

The Fisheries Act, 1986, addresses regulations for fishery management, conservation measures, registration of vessels and enforcement. The Act is focused on the larger and more economically significant marine fisheries. The use of poison for catching fish in both marine and freshwaters is prohibited under the Act. There is a provision under section 20 of the Act for the establishment of Fishing Priority Areas where "special measures are necessary to ensure that authorised fishing within the area is not impeded" and for the establishment of marine reserves under section 22. The administration of the Fisheries Act is carried out by the Fisheries Division of the Ministry of Agriculture, Forestry, Fisheries and Rural Transformation.

St. Vincent and the Grenadines is a signatory to several international conventions regarding conservation, including the UN Convention on Biological Diversity and The Convention on International Trade in Endangered Species. The Government produces regular reports on the Nation's progress towards the biodiversity goals outlined by the Convention on Biological Diversity; however, plans for the conservation of freshwater biodiversity are barely addressed (6th National Report to The UN Convention on Biological Diversity, Gov. SVG., 2019).

Conservation of freshwater biodiversity in St. Vincent and the Grenadines is impeded by-
- Overlapping and fragmented legislation.
- A mismatch of institutional resources to responsibilities regarding conservation of freshwater biodiversity.
- Lack of institutional and inter-sectoral communication regarding the conservation of freshwater biodiversity and management of their biological resources.

The above issues, in conjunction with lack of documented information regarding freshwater biodiversity, have resulted in a lack of institutional ownership and action on the conservation of freshwater biodiversity. Conservation planning has overlooked the river as a habitat and the biodiversity contained within it thus far.

SUGGESTED CONSERVATION RESPONSE:
- Rationalisation and clarification of the role the institutions involved in the management of freshwater resources and the conservation of freshwater biodiversity.
- The development of a national policy for the conservation of freshwater biodiversity and the sustainable management of traditional freshwater fisheries and preservation of their cultural heritage. This policy should be incorporated into future National Biodiversity Strategy and Action Plans for SVG.
- Put freshwater biodiversity on the agenda. The establishment of, or the activation of existing boards (the National Environmental Advisory Board) comprising of representatives of those bodies involved in freshwater management, to address the rationalisation of conservation roles and to formulate a freshwater biodiversity policy.
- Seek partnerships with research institutions and funding for the implementation of the conservation of freshwater biodiversity policy and scientific research and monitoring to inform successful implementation.

Conclusions

The present survey is the first comprehensive inventory of the freshwater and brackish water fish and decapod crustaceans found in St. Vincent W.I.

Eighteen species of freshwater and brackish water fish species, belonging to thirteen families, were recorded. Two species were first records in the literature for St. Vincent: the Mozambique tilapia, (*Oreochromis mossambicus*) and Busck's Stone-biting Goby (*Sicydium buscki*). Two species, previously recorded only from museum specimens collected in St. Vincent, were reported: the riverine clingfish (*Gobiesox cephalus*) and the guppy (*Poecilia reticulata*).

Thirteen species of freshwater and brackish water decapod crustaceans were recorded: ten shrimp species of three families, and three crab species of three families. One species was a first record in the literature for St. Vincent, the blue crab (*Callinectes sapidus*). The shrimp *Macrobrachium crenulatum* previously only recorded only from museum specimens collected in St. Vincent was reported.

Freshwater ecosystems are amongst the most globally threatened. The IUCN has assessed 28% of freshwater fish and 30% of freshwater crustaceans as threatened with extinction. The numerous and growing threats to freshwater fish and decapod crustaceans have been discussed in the Vincentian context. The diadromous life cycle of the majority of Vincentian freshwater fish and decapod crustaceans affords them resilience to local and temporary habitat disruptions. Damaged rivers can be recolonised from the sea by post-larvae originating from unaffected rivers. Widespread and general environmental degradation of the region's rivers poses a potential and increasing threat even to this resilient fauna.

Historically, policy makers have considered the rivers of St. Vincent primarily as a source of water for domestic, agricultural and industrial purposes, and for the generation of hydroelectricity. The "invisibility" of freshwater biodiversity to conservation planners in St. Vincent may be partially explained by the historic lack of published information about St. Vincent's species. In addition, traditional freshwater fisheries and the species that sustain them have often been overlooked and undervalued. With the publication of this inventory, the freshwater and brackish water fish and decapod crustacean species extant in St. Vincent are now known. This knowledge represents an important step towards the conservation of the St. Vincent's freshwater biodiversity.

Bibliography

Abele, L. 1992. A Review of the Grapsid Crab Genus Sesarma (Crustacea: Decapoda: Grapsidae) in America, with the Description of a New Genus. Smithsonian Contributions to Zoology. 527.

Abell, R., M. Thieme, C. Revenga, M. Bryer, M. Kottelat, N. Bogutskaya, B. Coad, N. Mandrak, S. Balderas, W. Bussing, M. Stiassny, P. Skelton, G. Allen, P. Unmack, A. Naseka, R. Ng, N. Sindorf, J. Robertson, E. Armijo, P. Petry, Paulo. 2008. Freshwater Ecoregions of the World: A New Map of Biogeographic Units for Freshwater Biodiversity Conservation. BioScience. 58. 403-414.

Adams, A., K. Guindon, A. Horodysky, T. MacDonald, R. McBride, J. Shenker, R. Ward. 2019. *Megalops atlanticus* (errata version published in 2020). *The IUCN Red List of Threatened Species* 2019. https://dx.doi.org/10.2305/IUCN.UK.2019-2.RLTS.T191823A174796143.en (Viewed 5/12/24)

Aiken, K.A. Reproduction, diet and population structure of the mountain mullet, Agonostomus monticola, in Jamaica, West Indies. *Environmental Biology of Fishes* **53**, 347–352 (1998).

Albertoni, E.F., C. Palma-Silva, F.A. Esteves,. 2003. Natural diet of three species of shrimp in a Tropical Coastal Lagoon. Brazilian Archives of Biology and Technology, 46: 395-403.

Albrecht, C., Clewing, C., Van Damme, D. & Lange, C. 2018. *Melanoides tuberculata. The IUCN Red List of Threatened Species* 2018. https://dx.doi.org/10.2305/IUCN.UK.2018-2.RLTS.T155675A120117210.en. (Viewed 5/13/24)

Almeida, A.O., A.P. Coelho, J.R. Luz, J.T.A dos Santos, N.R. Ferraz. 2008. Decapod crustaceans in fresh waters of southeastern Bahia, Brazil. Rev. biol. trop, San José, v. 56, n. 3, p. 1225-1254, Sept. 2008.

Anderson, W.D. Jr. 2003 Lutjanidae. Snappers. p. 1479-1504. In K.E. Carpenter (ed.) FAO species identification guide for fishery purposes. The living marine resources of the Western Central Atlantic. Vol. 3: Bony fishes part 2 (Opistognathidae to Molidae), sea turtles and marine mammals.

Anger, K., G. Torres, L. Gimenez, Luis. 2006. Metamorphosis of a sesarmid river crab, Armases roberti: Stimulation by adult odours versus inhibition by salinity stress. Marine and Freshwater Behaviour and Physiology - MAR FRESHW BEHAV PHYSIOL. 39. 269-278. Aquarium of the Pacific. Cane Toad. 2024. https://www.aquariumofpacific.org/onlinelearningcenter/species/cane_toad/#:~:text=Also%20known%20as%20the%20giant,parotid%20glands%20on%20each%20shoulder. (Viewed 5/13/24)

Ardon, D. & McMahan, C. 2020. Gobiesox cephalus. The IUCN Red List of Threatened Species 2020: https://dx.doi.org/10.2305/IUCN.UK.2020-2.RLTS.T168962425A170647178.en (Viewed on 5/10/24)

Avigliano E., A. Ibañez, N. Fabré, R. Fortunato, V. Méndez, A. Vicente, J. Pisonero, A. Volpedo. 2021. Unravelling the complex habitat use of the white mullet, Mugil curema, in several coastal environments from Neotropical Pacific and Atlantic waters. Aquatic Conservation Marine and Freshwater Ecosystems.

Barbeyron, C., E. Lefrancois, Estelle, D. Monti, P. Keith, C. Lord. 2017. Gardening behaviour of Sicydium punctatum (Gobioidei: Sicydiinae): in vitro experiments in the context of chlordecone pollution in Guadeloupe Island rivers. Cybium: international journal of ichthyology. 41. 85-92.

Barros-Alves, S., D.F.R. Alves, G. Hirose. 2021. Population biology of the freshwater shrimp Atya scabra (Leach, 1816) (Crustacea: Decapoda) in São Francisco River, Brazil: evidence from a population at risk of extinction. Nauplius. 29. 10.1590/2358-2936e2021009.
Bell K.N.I., page on: Gobies http://www.ucs.mun.ca/~kbell/goby/Intro.html accessed 17/12/23

Bell, K. N. I. 2009. What Comes Down Must Go Up: American Fisheries Society 2nd Symposium on Diadromous Fishes. (Invited speaker.)

Bell, K. N. I., J.A. Brown. 1995. Active salinity choice and enhanced swimming endurance in 0 to 8-d-old larvae of diadromous gobies, with emphasis on Sicydium punctatum (Pisces), in Dominica, West Indies. Mar. Biol. 121: 409-417.

BELL, K.N.I. 1994.Thesis: Life cycle, early life history, fisheries and recruitment dynamics of diadromous gobies of Dominica, W.I., emphasising *Sicydium punctatum* Perugia. Biology Department, Memorial University of Newfoundland. St. John's, Canada

Bell, K.N.I. 1999. An overview of goby-fry fisheries. Naga, The ICLARM quarterly. Vol 22

Benchetrit J., J. McCleave,. (2015). Current and historical distribution of the American eel Anguilla rostrata in the countries and territories of the Wider Caribbean. ICES Journal of Marine Science. 73.

Bertini, G., J. Baeza, E. Pérez. 2014. A test of large-scale reproductive migration in females of the amphidromous shrimp Macrobrachium acanthurus (Caridea : Palaemonidae) from south-eastern Brazil. Marine and Freshwater Research. 65.

Betts, J., J. Espinoza, J. Mayer, J. Christopher, U. Gerald, D. Armando. 2020. Fishing with Pesticides Affects River Fisheries and Community Health in the Indio Maíz Biological Reserve, Nicaragua. Sustainability. 12.

Bills, R. 2019. Oreochromis mossambicus (errata version published in 2020). The IUCN Red List of Threatened Species. https://dx.doi.org/10.2305/IUCN.UK.2019-3.RLTS.T63338A174782954.en (viewed on 5/9/24)

Bowles, D., K. Aziz, C. Knight, Charles. 2009. Macrobrachium (Decapoda: Caridea: Palaemonidae) in the Contiguous United States: A Review of the Species and an Assessment of Threats to Their Survival. Journal of Crustacean Biology. 20. 158-171.

Bragança, P., E. Guimarães, P. Brito, F. Ottoni, Felipe.2020. On the natural occurrence of Poecilia reticulata Peters, 1859 (Cyprinodontiformes: Poeciliidae). Cybium: International Journal of Ichthyology.

Burggren,W.W., B.R. McMahon. 1988. Biology of Land Crabs Cambridge University Press

Caribbean conservation Association. 1991. Country Environmental Profile, St. Vincent and the Grenadines. St. Michael, Barbados.

Casselman, P.C., J., Crook, V., DeLucia, M.-B., Jacoby, D. & Gollock, M. 2023. *Anguilla rostrata*. The IUCN Red List of Threatened Species 2023: e.T191108A129638652. https://dx.doi.org/10.2305/IUCN.UK.2023-1.RLTS.T191108A129638652.en. Accessed on 14 May 2024.

Castro, M.G., J.P. Vieira, R.J. Albieri, E. Mendonca, L. Villwock de Miranda, N.N. Fadre, M. Brick Peres, B. Padovani-Ferreira, F.M.S da Silva, A.T.M. Rodrigues, L. Chao, L. 2019. *Mugil curema*. The IUCN Red List of Threatened Species 2019. http://dx.doi.org/10.2305/IUCN.UK.2019-2.RLTS.T190168A82660284.en (Viewed 5/13/24)

Cervigón F R Cipriani, W. Fischer, L. Garibaldi, M.Hendrix, Lemus A.J.,Marquez R, Poutiers J.M., Robaina G., Rodriguez B, 1993 Field Guide to the Commrcial Marine and Brackish-Water Resources of the Northern Coast of South America, Food and Agriculture Organisation of the United Nations, Rome.

Chance, F.A., Hobbs, H.H. 1969. The freshwater and Terrestial Decaopd Crustaceans of the West Indies with Special Reference to Dominica. United States National Museum Bulletin 292. Smithsonian Institution Press Washington. D.C.

Ching, C.A. and Velez Jr, M.J., 1985. Mating, incubation and embryo number in the freshwater prawn Macrobrachium heterochirus (Wiegmann, 1836)(Decapoda, Palaemonidae) under laboratory conditions. *Crustaceana*, pp.42-48.

Choudhury, P. C. 1971b. Laboratory rearing of larvae of the palaemonid shrimp Macrobrachium acanthurus (Wiegmann, 1836). Crustaceana 21, 113–126.

Choudhury, P.C. 1971a. Complete Larval Development of the Palaemonid Shrimp Macrobrachium Carcinus (L.), Reared in the Laboratory (Decapoda, Palaemonidae). Crustaceana, 20(1), 51-69.

Clark, A.H. 1905. The habits of the West Indian Whitebait. The American Naturalist. May 1905, 39 (461). P 335-337.

Coat, S., D. Monti, C. Bouchon, G. Lepoint. 2009. Trophic relationships in a tropical stream food web assessed by stable isotope analysis. Freshwater Biology. 54. 1028 - 1041.

Coat, S., D. Monti, P. Legendre, C. Bouchon, F. Massat, G. Lepoint . 2011. Organochlorine pollution in tropical rivers (Guadeloupe): Role of ecological factors in food web bioaccumulation. Environ Pollut. 2011 Jun, 159 (6)

Cook, B., S. Bernays, C. Pringle, J. Hughes. 2009. Marine dispersal determines the genetic population structure of migratory stream fauna of Puerto Rico: Evidence for island-scale population recovery processes. Journal of the North American Benthological Society. 28.

Cooney, P., T. Kwak. 2013. Spatial Extent and Dynamics of Dam Impacts on Tropical Island Freshwater Fish Assemblages. BioScience. 63. 176-190.

Covich, A., T. Crowl. 2006. Effects of drought and hurricane disturbances on headwater distributions of palaemonid river shrimp (Macrobrachium spp.) in the Luquillo Mountains, Puerto Rico, Journal of the North American Benthological Society

Covich, A., T. Crowl, S. Johnson, D. Varza, D. Certain .1991. Post-Hurricane Hugo Increases in Atyid Shrimp Abundances in a Puerto Rican Montane Stream. Biotropica Vol. 23, No. 4, (Dec., 1991), pp. 448-454

Covich, A.P., T. A. Crowl, T. Heartsill-Scalley. 2006. Effects of drought and hurricane disturbances on headwater distributions of palaemonid river shrimp (Macrobrachium spp.) in the Luquillo Mountains, Puerto Rico. J. N. Am. Benthol. Soc., 2006, 25(1):99–107

Crabtree, R.E., E.C Cyr, J.M. Dean. 1995. Age and growth of tarpon, *Megalops atlanticus*, from south Florida waters. *Fish. Bull. 93(4)*: 619-628

Crowl, T., V. Welsh, T. Heartsill-Scalley, A. Covich. 2006. Effects of different types of conditioning on rates of leaf-litter shredding by Xiphocaris elongata, a Neotropical freshwater shrimp. Journal of The North American Benthological Society - J N AMER BENTHOL SOC. 25. 198-208.

Cruz, G.A. 1987. Reproductive biology and feeding habits of cuyamel joturus pichardi and tepemechin agonostomus monticola pisces mugilidae from rio platano mosquitia Honduras Cruz, G.A. Bulletin of Marine Science 40(1): 63-72 1987

Cruz-Soltero, S., D.E. Alston. 1992 Status Report on Research with Atya lanipes and Atya scabra in Puerto Rico. Proceedings of the 42 Gulf and Caribbean Fisheries Institute. University of Puerto Rico.

Cumberlidge, N. 2008. Guinotia dentata. The IUCN Red List of Threatened Species 2008: http://dx.doi.org/10.2305/IUCN.UK.2008.RLTS.T134595A3983694.en (Viewed 5/13/24)

Davis, B. 2016. From the Bay and Back Again: The lifecycle of the blue crab Maryland Natural Resource magazine, Vol. 19, No. 2 https://news.maryland.gov/dnr/2016/03/20/crab-lifecycle/#:~:text=It%20takes%20about%2031%2D49,into%20the%20first%20crab%20stage (Viewed 5/13/24)

Dawson, C.E., 1984. Revision of the genus *Microphis* Kaup (Pisces: Syngnathidae). Bull. Mar. Sci. 35(2):117-181.

De Grave, S. 2013. Jonga serrei. The IUCN Red List of Threatened Species 2013: http://dx.doi.org/10.2305/IUCN.UK.2013-1.RLTS.T198276A2518602.en (Viewed 5/13/24)

De Grave, S. 2013. Macrobrachium acanthurus. The IUCN Red List of Threatened Species 2013: http://dx.doi.org/10.2305/IUCN.UK.2013-1.RLTS.T198030A2509166.en (Viewed 5/13/24)

De Grave, S. 2013. Macrobrachium carcinus. The IUCN Red List of Threatened Species 2013: http://dx.doi.org/10.2305/IUCN.UK.2013-1.RLTS.T198003A2508328.en (Viewed 5/13/24)

De Grave, S. 2013. Macrobrachium crenulatum. The IUCN Red List of Threatened Species 2013: http://dx.doi.org/10.2305/IUCN.UK.2013-1.RLTS.T198116A2512372.en (Viewed 5/13/24)

De Grave, S. 2013. Macrobrachium faustinum. The IUCN Red List of Threatened Species. http://dx.doi.org/10.2305/IUCN.UK.2013-1.RLTS.T197761A2498944.en (Viewed 5/13/24)

De Grave, S. 2013. Macrobrachium heterochirus. The IUCN Red List of Threatened Species 2013: e.T197727A2497668. http://dx.doi.org/10.2305/IUCN.UK.2013-1.RLTS.T197727A2497668.en (Viewed 5/13/24)

De Grave, S. 2013. Micratya poeyi. The IUCN Red List of Threatened Species 2013: http://dx.doi.org/10.2305/IUCN.UK.2013-1.RLTS.T197667A2495277.en (Viewed 5/13/24)

De Grave, S. 2013. Xiphocaris elongata. The IUCN Red List of Threatened Species 2013: http://dx.doi.org/10.2305/IUCN.UK.2013-1.RLTS.T197701A2496628.en (Viewed 5/13/24)

De Grave, S., F. Mantelatto, F. Alvarez, J. Villalobos. 2013. Atya innocous. The IUCN Red List of Threatened Species 2013: http://dx.doi.org/10.2305/IUCN.UK.2013-1.RLTS.T197934A2505662.en (Viewed 5/24/24)

De Grave, S., J. Villalobos, F. Mantelatto, F.Alvarez. 2013. Atya scabra. The IUCN Red List of Threatened Species 2013: http://dx.doi.org/10.2305/IUCN.UK.2013-1.RLTS.T197895A2504208.en (Viewed 5/24/24)

Deacon, A., A. Magurran, Anne. 2016. How Behaviour Contributes to the Success of an Invasive Poeciliid Fish: The Trinidadian Guppy (Poecilia reticulata) as an Invasive Species. In PressEditors: Judith Weis, Daniel Sol. Biological Invasions and Animal Behaviour (pp.266-290) Chapter: 15, Publisher: Cambridge University

Deacon, A., CABI Compendium Poecilia reticulata 2023. https://www.cabidigitallibrary.org/doi/10.1079/cabicompendium.68208 (Viewed 5/13/24)

Díaz, F., E. Sierra, A. D. Re, L. Rodríguez. 2002. Behavioural thermoregulation and critical thermal limits of Macrobrachium acanthurus (Wiegman) Journal of Thermal Biology Volume 27, Issue 5, October 2002, Pages 423-428.

Diesel R, Schuh M. 1998. Effects of salinity and starvation on larval development of the crabs Armases ricordi and A. roberti (Decapoda: Grapsidae) from Jamaica, with notes on the biology and ecology of adults. J. Crustacean Biol. 18:423-436

Dudgeon, D., A.H. Arthington, M.O. Gessner, Z. Kawabata, D.J. Knowler, C. Lévêque, R.J. Naiman, A.H. Prieur-Richard, D. Soto, M.L. Stiassny, C.A. Sullivan. Freshwater biodiversity: importance, threats, status and conservation challenges. Biol Rev Camb Philos Soc. 2006 May;81(2):163-82.

Dussault, G.V., D.L. Kramer. 1981. Food and Feeding Behavior of the Guppy, Poecilia reticulata (Pisces: Poeciliidae), Can. j. Zool., 1981, vol. 59, no. 4, pp. 684–701.

Egse, C.K., G.H. Bolstad, G. Rosenquist, J.A. Endler, C. Pélabon. 2011. Geographical variation in allometry in the guppy (Poecilia reticulata) Journal of Evolutionary Biology Volume24, Issue12 December 2011, Pages 2631-2638

Engman, A. C., T. J. Kwak, J. R. Fischer. 2017. Recruitment phenology and pelagic larval duration in Caribbean amphidromous fishes. Freshwater Science 36(4):851–865.

Engman, A., G. Hogue, W. Starnes, M. Raley, T. Kwak. 2019. Puerto Rico Sicydium goby diversity: species-specific insights on population structures and distributions. Neotropical Biodiversity. 5. 22-29.

Engman, A., T. Kwak, J. Fischer. 2021. Big runs of little fish: First estimates of run size and exploitation in an amphidromous postlarvae fishery. Canadian Journal of Fisheries and Aquatic Sciences. 78.

Environmental Resources Management, 2016, St. Vincent Geothermal Project Environmental and Social Impact Assessment
https://www.caribank.org/publication_types/environmental-and-social-impact-assessments/st-vincent-geothermal-project-phase-1 (Viewed 5/13/24)

Erdman, D. S. 1961. Notes on the biology of the gobiid fish Sicydium plumieri in Puerto Rico, Bulletin of Marine Science Volume 11, Number 1, 1961, pp. 448-456

FAO Fisheries and Aquaculture Department. 2023. Species Fact Sheets Oreochromis mossambicus (Peters, 1852)
https://www.fao.org/figis/pdf/fishery/species/2408/en?title=FAO%20Fisheries%20%26amp%3B%20Aquaculture%20-%20Aquatic%20species (Viewed 5/14/24)

Felgenhauer, B.E., L.G. Abele. 1982. Aspects of the Mating Behavour in the tropical Freshwater Shrimp Atya innocous (Herbst). Biotropica, Vol 14, No.4, 296-300

Fievet, E., S. Dolédec, P. Lim. 2001. Distribution of migratory fishes and shrimps along multivariate gradients in tropical island streams. Journal of Fish Biology. 59. 390 - 402.

Fofonoff P.W., G.M. Ruiz, B. Steves, C. Simkanin C, J.T. Carlton JT. 2018. Oreochromis mossambicus. National Exotic Marine and Estuarine Species Information System. https://invasions.si.edu/nemesis/species_summary/170015 (viewed on 2/7/24)

Forks, K., M. Hopkins, S. Veillon, W. Whitney. 2014 The Diet of the freshwater clingfish, Gobiesox cephalus (Teleostei: Gobiesocidae),Texas A&M University, College Station, USA.

Frias-Torres, S. 2002 Oceanic Transport and Life History of the Tropical Western Atlantic Opossum Pipefish, Microphis brachyurus lineatus. Ph D Thesis. Florida Tech, Melbourne, Florida, USA.

Froese, R. and D. Pauly. Editors. 2024. FishBase. World Wide Web electronic publication. www.fishbase.org (Viewed 5/24)

Frotté, L., J. Ringelstein, D. Monti, M. Robert, C. Pécheyran, N. Améziane, H.Tabouret. 2019. Detection of full and limited amphidromous migratory dynamics of fish in Caribbean rivers. Ecology of Freshwater Fish. 29.

Fryer, G. 1977a. Studies on the Functional Morphology and Ecology of the Atyid Prawns of Dominica. Volume 277, Issue 952 of Philosophical transactions of the Royal Society of London, 25th Feb 1977

Fryer, G. 1977b. The Atyid Prawns Of Dominica. Forty-fifth annual report for the year ended 31st March 1977. Freshwater Biological Association, Ambleside

Galvão, R., S.L.S. Bueno. 2000. Population structure and reproductive biology of the camacuto shrimp, Atya scabra (Decapoda, Caridea, Atyidae), from São Sebastião, Brazil. Crust. Issues 12: 291-299

Gamba, A. 1982. Macrobrachium: its presence in estuaries of the northern Venezuelan coast (Decapoda, Palaemonidae). Carib. J. Sci. 18: 23-25, figs.1-4: 135-136.

García-Guerrero, M., F. Becerril-Morales, F. Vega-Villasante, L. Espinosa-Chaurand. 2013. The Macrobrachium prawns with economic and fisheries importance in latin America: Present knowledge, ecological role, and conservation. Latin American Journal of Aquatic Research. 41. 651-675.

GBIF Secretariat (2023). GBIF Backbone Taxonomy. *Macrobrachium crenulatum* Holthuis, 1950.Checklist dataset https://doi.org/10.15468/39omei accessed via GBIF.org (Viewed 1/28/24)

GBIF Secretariat (2023). *Nerine punctulata* (Lamarck, 1816) GBIF Backbone Taxonomy. Checklist dataset https://doi.org/10.15468/39omei (Viewed 5/13/24)

GBIF Secretariat. 2023. *Sicydium punctatum (Perugia, 1896)*. GBIF Backbone Taxonomy. https://www.gbif.org/occurrence/search?q=sicydium%20%20punctatum%20st.vincent%20and%20the%20grenadines) (viewed 5/14/23)

GBIF Secretariat. *Dajaus monticola* (Bancroft, 1834). 2023. GBIF Backbone Taxonomy. Checklist dataset https://doi.org/10.15468/39omei accessed via GBIF.org on 2023-11-15.

GBIF Secretariat. *Microphis lineatus* (Kaup, 1856).2023. GBIF Backbone Taxonomy. https://www.gbif.org/es/species/5712327 (Viewed 5/13/24)

GBIF Secretariat: *Armases roberti* Occurance down load: https://www.gbif.org/occurrence/1318028929 (Viewed 5/15/24)

GBIF Secretariat: GBIF Backbone Taxonomy. *Gobiesox cephalus* https://www.gbif.org/occurrence/gallery?q=gobiesox%20cephalus (viewed on 5/10/24)

GBIF Secretariat: *Guinotia dentata* Occurance down load: https://www.gbif.org/occurrence/1319478762 (Viewed 5/15/24)

GBIF Secretariat: Poecelia reticulata Occurance down load: https://www.gbif.org/occurrence/search?q=poecilia%20reticulata%20st.%20vincent%20and%20the%20grenadines (Viewed 5/15/24)

Gidmark, N.J., K. Pos, B. Matheson, E. Ponce, M.W. Westneat. 2019. Functional Morphology and Biomechanics of Feeding in Fishes. In: Bels, V., Whishaw, I. (eds) Feeding in Vertebrates. Fascinating Life Sciences. Springer, Cham.

Gilmore, G., 2009. Species of Concern NOAA National Marine Fisheries Service. Opossum pipefish https://www.nrc.gov/docs/ML1224/ML12240A312.pdf (Viewed 5/13/24)

Gomes, A.F.T., E. Mossolin, F. Mantelatto, Fernando. 2012. Populational and Reproductive Aspects of Southern Macrobrachium acanthurus (Wiegmann, 1836) (Crustacea: Palaemonidae), Brazil.. Brazilian Journal of Aquatic Science and Technology.16.

Gomes-Silva, G., E. Cyubahiro, T. Wronski, R. Riesch, M. Plath. 2020. Water pollution affects fish community structure and alters evolutionary trajectories of invasive guppies (Poecilia reticulata). Science of the Total Environment, 730.

Gonzalez, J. G., T. Frédou, P.J. Duarte-Neto, C. Petit, M. Labonne, R.P. Lessa, A.M. Darnaude. 2022. Age validation and growth in an exploited but poorly studied tropical fish species, the horse-eye jack (Caranx latus). Fisheries Research, 253

Government of St. Vincent and the Grenadines. August 2021. La Soufriere Volcanic Eruption Sector Reports https://reliefweb.int/sites/reliefweb.int/files/resources/Full%20Report%20SVG%20PDNA%20Volcanic%20Eruption.pdf (Viewed 5/13/24)

Government of Saint Vincent and the Grenadines January 16, 2014 Rapid Damage and LossAssessment (DaLA) December 24-25, 2013 Floods

Government of St. Vincent and the Grenadies. Central Water and Sewage Authority Act. 1991. https://www.fao.org/faolex/results/details/en/c/LEX-FAOC048934/ (viewed 9/29/24)

Government of St. Vincent and the Grenadies. The Fisheries Act. 1986. https://faolex.fao.org/docs/pdf/stv2112.pdf (viewed 9/29/24)

Government of St. Vincent and the Grenadies. The Forest Resource Conservation Act. 1992. https://www.fao.org/faolex/results/details/en/c/LEX-FAOC175207/#:~:text=This%20Act%20provides%20with%20respect,and%20lease%20of%20forest%20land (viewed 9/29/24)

Government of St. Vincent and the Grenadies. Ministry of Health, Wellness and the Environment Web Page. 2024. https://health.gov.vc/health/index.php/environmental-health (viewed 9/29/24)

Government of St. Vincent and the Grenadies. Sixth national Biodiversity Action Plan Repoort to the Convention on Biological Diversity. 2019. https://www.cbd.int/doc/nr/nr-06/vc-nr-06-en.pdf (viewed 9/29/24)

Government of St. Vincent and the Grenadies. The National Parks Act. 2002. https://www.fao.org/faolex/results/details/en/c/LEX-FAOC077976/ (viewed 9/29/24)

Government of St. Vincent and the Grenadies. The Wildlife Protection Act. 1987.

https://www.fao.org/faolex/results/details/en/c/LEX-FAOC005746/ (viewed 9/29/24)

Government of St. Vincent and the Grenadies.. Ministry of Finance, Economic Planning and Information Technology Web Page. 2024.
https://finance.gov.vc/finance/index.php/central (viewed 9/29/24)

Government of St. Vincent and the Grenadines. Ministry of Agriculture, Forestry, Fisheries, Rural transformation, Industry and Labour. Web Page "Legal and Regulatory Framework" https://agriculture.gov.vc/agriculture/index.php?option=com_content&view=article&id=374&Itemid=350 (Viewed 4/29/24)

Graham R., D.W. Castellanos. 2005. Courtship and spawning behaviors of carangid species in Belize. Fishery Bulletin- National Oceanic and Atmospheric Administration. 103. 426-43

Gran, K.B., D.R. Montgomery. 2005. Spatial and temporal patterns in fluvial recovery following volcanic eruptions: Channel response to basin-wide sediment loading at Mount Pinatubo, Philippines. *GSA Bulletin* 2005;; 117 (1-2): 195–211. Gran, K.B., D.R. Montgomery. 2005. Spatial and temporal patterns in fluvial recovery following volcanic eruptions: Channel response to basin-wide sediment loading at Mount Pinatubo, Philippines. *GSA Bulletin* 2005;; 117 (1-2): 195–211.

Grandgirard, V., D. Monti, P. Valade, N. Lamouroux, J. P. Mallet, H. Grondin. 2014. Hydraulic preferences of shrimps and fishes in tropical insular rivers. River Research and Applications, 30 (6),p. 766-p. 779.

Greathouse, E., J. March, C. Pringle. 2005. Recovery of a tropical stream after a harvest-related chlorine poisoning event. Freshwater Biology. 50. 603 - 615.

Guazzelli Gonzalez, Júlio & Darnaude, Audrey & Duarte-Neto, Paulo & Le Loc'h, François & Lima, Mayara & Ménard, Frédéric & Ferreira, Valdimere & Lucena Frédou, Flavia & Munaron, Jean-Marie & Fredou, Thierry. (2021). Trophic ecology of the juveniles of two jack species (Caranx latus and C. hippos) in contrasted tropical estuaries. Estuarine, Coastal and Shelf Science. 255. 107370. 10.1016/j.ecss.2021.107370.
Guilding, L. 1823. An Account of some rare West Indian Crustacea. Transactions of the Linnean Society of London 1825; 14: 334-338

Hagood, R., S. Willis. 1976. Cost comparisons of rearing larvae of freshwater shrimp, Macrobrachium acanthurus and M. rosenbergii to juveniles. Aquaculture, 1976, *7, 59-74*.

Harris, N., J. Neal, J., P. Perschbacher, C. Mace, M. Muñoz-Hincapié. 2011. Notes on hatchery spawning methods for bigmouth sleeper Gobiomorus dormitor. Aquaculture Research. 42.

Harrison A.D., J.J. Rankin. 1976a. Hydrobiological Studies of the Eastern Lesser Antillean Islands I. St. Vincent Freshwater habitats and water chemistry. Arch. Hydrobiol./Suppl. 50, 1, 96-144

Harrison A.D., J.J. Rankin. 1976b. Hydrobiological Studies of the Eastern Lesser Antillean Islands II. St. Vincent Freshwater fauna – its distribution, tropical river zonation and biogeography. Arch. Hydrobiol./Suppl. 50, 2/3. 275-311

Harrison, I. J. 2002. Mugilidae. In K.E. Carpenter (ed.) FAO species identification guide for fishery purposes. The living marine resources of the Western Central Atlantic. Vol.2. 1071-1085

HERNÁNDEZ-GÓMEZ, R. E., R. RODILES-HERNÁNDEZ, M. MENDOZA-CARRANZA, I. VALENZUELA-CÓRDOVA, M. PERERA-GARCÍA. 2021 Record of Rhonciscus crocro (Cuvier, 1830) (Haemulidae: Haemulinae) in the Usumacinta River, Mexico. Fishtaxa-Journal of Fish Taxonomy . 2021, Issue 22, p16-22.

Herrera-Correal, J., E.C. Mossolin, Emerson, I.S. Wehrtmann, F.L. Mantelatto. 2013. Reproductive aspects of the caridean shrimp Atya scabra (Leach, 1815) (Decapoda: Atyidae) in São Sebastião Island, southwestern Atlantic, Brazil Latin American Journal of Aquatic Research, vol. 41, núm. 4, septiembre-, 2013, pp. 676-684

Hobbs, H.H., C. W. Hart. 1982. The Shrimp Genus Atya (Decapoda: Atyidae). Issue 364 of Smithsonian contributions to zoology, Smithsonian Institution Press, Washington, USA.

Holthuis, L.B. 1950. Preliminary descriptions of twelve new species of palaemonid prawns from American waters (Crustacea Decapoda). Proceedings, van de Koninklijke Nederlandsche Akademie van Wetenschappen. 53: 93-99.

Holthuis, L.B. 1980. FAO Species catalogue. Vol. 1. Shrimps and prawns of the world. An annotated catalogue of species of interest to fisheries. FAO, Rome.

Hunte W., R. Mahon. 1983 Life History and Exploitation of Macrobrachium faustinum in a Tropical High-Gradient River. FISHERY BULLETIN, Vol. 81, No. 3

Hunte, W. 1977. Laboratory rearing of the atyid shrimps Atya innocous Herbst and Micratya poeyi Guerin-Meneville (Decapoda, Atyidae) Aquaculture Volume 11, Issue 4, August 1977, Pages 373-378

Hunte, W. 1979. The rediscovery of the freshwater shrimp Macrobrachium crenulatum in Jamaica. Studies on the Fauna of Curaçao and other Caribbean Islands, 58(1), 69–74.

Hunte, W. 2008. The distribution of freshwater shrimps (Atyidae and Palaemonidae) in Jamaica. Zoological Journal of the Linnean Society.64. 135-150.

Ismael, D., G.S. Moreira. 1997. Effect of temperature and salinity on respiratory rate and development of early larval stages of Macrobrachium acanthurus (Wiegmann, 1836) (Decapoda, Palaemonidae). Volume 118, Issue 3, November 1997, Pages 871-876

IUCN 2024. The IUCN Red List of Threatened Species. Version 2023-1. https://www.iucnredlist.org (Viewed 5/27/24)

IUCN SSC Amphibian Specialist Group. 2023. Rhinella marina. The IUCN Red List of Threatened Species 2023: https://dx.doi.org/10.2305/IUCN.UK.2023-1.RLTS.T100099625A2951416.en (Viewed 5/13/24)

Jacoby, D., J. Casselman, M. DeLucia, M. Gollock. 2017. *Anguilla rostrata.* The IUCN Red List of Threatened Species 2017 https://www.iucnredlist.org/species/191108/121739077 http://dx.doi.org/10.2305/IUCN.UK.2017-3.RLTS.T191108A121739077.en

Johnson, S., A. Covich, Alan. 2000. The importance of night-time observation for determining habitat preferences of stream biota. Regulated Rivers-research & Management -16. 91-99

Kadjo, V., O. Etchian, C. Ble, D. Soro, J. Yapi, A. Otchoumou. 2016. Caractérisation de la pêche aux crevettes d'eau douce Atya scabra (Leach, 1815) (Decapoda: Atyidae) dans la rivière Bia, Côte d'Ivoire. International Journal of Biological and Chemical Sciences. 10. 620.

Kikkert, D., T. Crowl, A. Covich, Alan. 2009. Upstream migration of amphidromous shrimps in the Luquillo Experimental Forest, Puerto Rico: Temporal patterns and environmental cues. Journal of The North American Benthological Society 28.

Kwak T.J., A.C Engman, C.G. Lilystrom. 2019 Ecology and conservation of the American eel in the Caribbean region Fisheries Management and Ecology.Vol 26, 1, p42-45

Lara, Luis. 2009. Reproductive Biology of the Freshwater Shrimp Macrobrachium Carcinus (L.) (Decapoda: Palaemonidae) from Costa Rica, Central America. Journal of Crustacean Biology. 29. 343-349.

Laughlin, R.A., 1982. Feeding habits of the blue crab, Callinectes sapidus Rathbun, in the Apalachicola estuary, Florida. *Bulletin of Marine Science*, *32*(4), pp.807-822.

Lefrancois, E., S. Coat, G. Lepoint, N. Vachiery, O. Gros, D. Monti. 2011. Epilithic biofilm as a key factor for small-scale river fisheries on Caribbean islands. Fisheries Management and Ecology. 18. 211 - 220.

Lima, J., J. Garcia, S. Thibério. 2014. Natural diet and feeding habits of a freshwater prawn (Macrobrachium carcinus: Crustacea, Decapoda) in the estuary of the Amazon River. Acta Amazonica. 44. 235-244.

Lindeman, K., W. Anderson, B. Padovani-Ferreira, J. Cowan, G. Sedberry, R. Claro, L.A. Rocha. 2019. Pomadasys crocro. The IUCN Red List of Threatened Species 2019: e.T192939A86333867. http://dx.doi.org/10.2305/IUCN.UK.2019-2.RLTS.T192939A86333867.en

Lochmann, S.E , C.M. Adelsberger, W. J. Neal. 2015 MOVEMENT OF BIGMOUTH SLEEPER, GOBIOMORUS DORMITOR, IN THE RÍO CAÑAS, PUERTO RICO, REVEALED BY RADIO TELEMETRY, AND A DISCUSSION OF THE SPECIES' AMPHIDROMOUS CHARACTERIZATION. Gulf and Caribbean Research Vol 26, 1-8

Loop News. 4th March 2024. US charges 2 Dominicans for smuggling American Eels in Puerto Rico
https://caribbean.loopnews.com/content/us-charges-2-dominicans-smuggling-american-eels-puerto-rico (Viewed 5/13/24)

Loria, L. 1993 Status Report On Caribbean Aquaculture. FOOD AND AGRICULTURE ORGANIZATION OF THE UNITED NATIONS Mexico City, FAO
https://www.fao.org/4/ab490e/AB490E04.htm

Lyons, T.J. 2021. *Poecilia reticulata*. *The IUCN Red List of Threatened Species* 2021: https://dx.doi.org/10.2305/IUCN.UK.2021-1.RLTS.T60444A3100119.en. (Viewed 5/13/24)

Mac Gregor R., J.M. Casselman, W.A. Allen. 2009. Natural Heritage, Anthropogenic Impacts, and Biopolitical Issues Related to the Status and Sustainable Management of American Eel: A Retrospective Analysis and Management Perspective at the Population Level. American Fisheries Society Symposium 69:713–740

Mai, A., S. Mauricio, L. Valéria, V. João. 2018. Discrimination of habitat use between two sympatric species of mullets, Mugil curema and Mugil liza (Mugiliformes: Mugilidae) in the rio Tramandaí Estuary, determined by otolith chemistry. Neotropical Ichthyology. 2

Mantelatto, F.L., A.F. Tamburus, T. Magalhães, R.C. Buranelli, M. Terossi, M. Negri, A.L. Castilho, R.C. Costa, F. Zara, F, J, Plazi. 2020. Checklist of decapod crustaceans from the coast of the São Paulo state (Brazil) supported by integrative molecular and morphological data: III. Infraorder Brachyura Latreille, 1802. Zootaxa. 2020 Nov 6; 48722

March, J.G., J.P. Benstead, C. M. Pringle, M. W. Ruebel. 2001. Linking shrimp assemblages with rates of detrital processing along an elevational gradient in a tropical stream Canadian Journal of Fisheries and Aquatic Sciences March 2001

Mares, F., (5/19/2400) Mexico City Congress Makes Rainwater harvesting Constitutional. Mexico Business News. https://mexicobusiness.news/infrastructure/news/mexico-city-congress-makes-rainwater-harvesting-constitutional (Viewed 5/28/24)

McMahan C.D., D. J. Elías, Y. Li, O. Domínguez-Domínguez, S. Rodriguez-Machado, A. Morales-Cabrera, D. Velásquez-Ramírez, K. R. Piller, P. Chakrabarty, W. A. Matamoros. 2021 Molecular systematics of the Awaous banana complex (River Gobies; Teleostei: Oxudercidae). Jounrnal of Fish Biology may 2021

McMahan, C., E. Diego, Y. Li, O. Domínguez-Domínguez, S. Rodríguez-Machado, C. Morales, A Cabrera, D. Velásquez,D. Ramírez, K. Piller, P. Chakrabarty, W. Matamoros, Wilfredo. 2021. Molecular systematics of the Awaous banana complex (River Gobies; Teleostei: Oxudercidae). Journal of Fish Biology. 99.

Mejía-Ortíz, L., F. Alvarez, R. Román, J. Viccon-Pale. 2001. Fecundity and distribution of freshwater prawns of the genus Macrobrachium in the Huitzilapan river, Veracruz, Mexico. Crustaceana. 74. 69-77.

Meyer-Rochow V.B., W.A. Ried, M. Haley. 1992. Photochemical Receptors in the Eye of the Jamaican Freshwater Shrimp Macrobrachium heterochirus. Researches on Crustaceans 21 (1992): 33-45

Miculka, B. 2009. Burrowing Habits, Habitat Selections, and Behaviors of Four Common Dominican Land Crabs; Guinotia dentata, Gecarcinus lateralis, Gecarcinus ruricola, and Cardisoma guanhumi. Texas A&M University

Milliken M.R., A.B. Williams. 1984. Synopsis *of* biological data *on the* blue crab, callinectes sapidus Rathbun. NOAA technical report NMFS ; 1.

Miranda-Marure, M., J. Martínez-Pérez, J. 2004. Reproductive Biology of the Opossum Pipefish, Microphis brachyurus lineatus, in Tecolutla Estuary, Veracruz, Mexico. Gulf and Caribbean Research.

Mobray, A., 2004. US Forest Service, El Yunque National Forest Page https://www.fs.usda.gov/detail/elyunque/learning/nature-science/?cid=stelprdb5302597 (Viewed 1/15/24)

Monti D., P. Keith, E. Vigneux. 2010. Atlas des poisson er des crustacés d'eau douce de la Guadeloupe. Muséum national d'Histoire Naturelle, Paris.

Monti, D., E. Lefrancois, C. Lord, J. Mortillaro, P. Lopez, Philippe K. 2018. Selectivity on epilithic diatom consumption for two tropical sympatric gobies: Sicydium punctatum Perugia, 1986 and Sicydium plumieri (Bloch, 1786). Cybium 2018, 42(4): 365-373

Morandi, B., A. Rivière-Honegger, C. Marylise. 2018. La pêche en rivière en Martinique quels sont les enjeux d'une patrimonialisation socio-environnementale . Études caribéennes. 41.

Moura R.L., Francini-Filho R.L., Chaves M.L., Minte-Vera C.V., Lindeman K. 2011. Use of riverine through reef habitat systems by dog snapper (Lutjanus jocu) in eastern Brazil Estuarine, Coastal and Shelf Science, Volume 95, Issue 1, 1 November 2011, Pages 274-278

Multigner L., P. Kadhel, F. Rouget, P. Blanchet, S. Cordier. 2016. Chlordecone exposure and adverse effects in French West Indies populations Environ Sci Pollut Res Int. 2016; 23: 3–8.

Murdy E.O., D. F. Hoese. 2002. In book: The Living Marine Resources of the Western Central Atlantic Vol.3 Bony fishes part 2 (Opistognathidae to Molidae) (pp.1781-1796)Chapter: Suborder Gobioidei - Gobiidae (gobies)Publisher: Food and Agriculture Organization of the United NationsEditors: Kent E. Carpenter

Murdy, E., J.L. Van Tassell. 2010. *Sicydium plumieri. The IUCN Red List of Threatened Species 2010* http://dx.doi.org/10.2305/IUCN.UK.20104.RLTS.T155188A4739603.en

Museums Victoria Staff .2010. Ferrissia Freshwater Limpet in Museums Victoria Collections https://collections.museumsvictoria.com.au/species/8507 (Viewed 3/5/24)

Myers, G. S. 1949. Salt-Tolerance of Fresh-Water Fish Groups in Relation to Zoogeographical Problems. Bijdragen tot de Dierkunde, 28(1), 315-322.

Nash, L.N., P.A.P. Antiqueira, G. Q. Romero, P. M. de Omena, P. Kratina. 2021. Warming of aquatic ecosystems disrupts aquatic-terrestrial linkages in the tropics. J Anim Ecol. 2021 Jul;90(7):1623-1634

NatureServe & Lyons, T.J. 2019. *Dajaus monticola*. The IUCN Red List of Threatened Species 2019:
 http://dx.doi.org/10.2305/IUCN.UK.2019-2.RLTS.T192943A129628295.en   (Viewed 5/13/24)

NatureServe, Sparks, J.S., T.J. Lyons. 2019. Microphis brachyurus. The IUCN Red List of

Threatened Species 2019: http://dx.doi.org/10.2305/IUCN.UK.20192.RLTS.T181547A130020921.en (Viewed 5/13/25)

Nordlie, F. 2012. Life-history characteristics of eleotrid fishes of the western hemisphere, and perils of life in a vanishing environment. Reviews in Fish Biology and Fisheries - REV FISH BIOL FISHERIES. 22.

Nordlie, F.G. 1981. Feeding and reproductive biology of eleotrid fishes in a tropical estuary. J. Fish Biol (1981) 18, 97-110

Ocasio-Torres M.E., T. Giray, T.A. Crowl, A.M. Sabat. 2015. Antipredator defence mechanism in the amphidromous shrimp Xiphocaris elongata (Decapoda: Xiphocarididae): rostrum length, Journal of Natural History, 49:25-26.
Ogden J. 1970. Relative Abundance, Food Habits, and Age of the American Eel, Anguilla rostrata (LeSueur), in Certain New Jersey Streams. Transactions of The American Fisheries Society - TRANS AMER FISH SOC. 99. 54-59.

Olivieri-Velázquez, K., J. Neal. 2018. Effects of Temperature and Salinity on Early Ontogeny of Bigmouth Sleeper Larvae. North American Journal of Aquaculture. 80. 42-51.

Orrell, Thomas. 2003. CENTROPOMIDAE. In book: The living marine resources of the Western Central Atlantic. Vol. 2. Bony fishes part 1 (Acipenseridae to Grammatidae) (pp.1286-1293) Edition: FAO Species Identification Guide for Fishery Purposes an American Society of Ichthyologists and Herpetologists Special Publication No. 5. Rome, FAO Chapter: SnooksPublisher: FOOD AND AGRICULTURE ORGANIZATION OF THE UNITED NATIONS Editors: K.E. Carpenter.

Palomares, M.L.D., D. Pauly. Editors. 2023. SeaLifeBase. Callinectes sapidus https://www.sealifebase.ca/Country/CountryList.php?ID=26794&GenusName=Callinectes& (Viewed 5/13/24)

Palomares, M.L.D., D. Pauly. Editors. 2024. SeaLifeBase..World Wide Web electronic publication.www.sealifebase.org, version (03/2024).

Pezold, F. 2015. Sicydium punctatum. The IUCN Red List of Threatened Species 2015. http://dx.doi.org/10.2305/IUCN.UK.2015-2.RLTS.T186056A1808598.en (Viewed 5/14/24)

Pezold, F., B. Cage. 2002. A review of the spinycheek sleepers, genus Eleotris (Teleostei: Eleotridae), of the Western Hemisphere, with comparison to the West African species. Tulane Studies in Zoology and Botany. 31. 19-63.

Pezold, F., J. van Tassell, K.A. Aiken, L. Tornabene, J. Bouchereau, J. 2019. Eleotris perniger. The IUCN Red List of Threatened Species 2019: http://dx.doi.org/10.2305/IUCN.UK.2019-2.RLTS.T185990A82653082.en (Viewed on 5/10/24)

Pezold, F., J. van Tassell, L. Tornabene, K. A. Aiken, J.L. Bouchereau. 2019. Awaous banana. The IUCN Red List of Threatened Species 2019: https://dx.doi.org/10.2305/IUCN.UK.2019-2.RLTS.T192933A2180099.en. (Viewed on 12 May 2024)

Pezold, F.,J. van Tassell, K. Aiken, L. Tornabene, J. Bouchereau, J. 2019. *Gobiomorus dormitor*. The IUCN Red List of Threatened Species 2019. http://dx.doi.org/10.2305/IUCN.UK.2019-2.RLTS.T186008A82656935.en

Phillip, D. 2017. Of Islands and Continents: The Storey of Freshwater Fish. Presentation at Caribaea Initiative. http://caribaea.org/wordpress/wp-content/uploads/PHILLIP-Dawn_RCW2017.pdf (Viewed 5/13/24)

Phillip, D. A. T. 1993. Reproduction and feeding of the mountain mullet, Agonostomus monticola, in Trinidad, West Indies. Environmental Biology of Fishes. 37. 47-55.

Pileggi, L. G., N. Rossi, I.S. Wehrtmann, F.L. Mantelatto. 2014. Molecular perspective on the American transisthmian species of Macrobrachium (Caridea, Palaemonidae). ZooKeys, 457, 109–131.

Pollom, R. 2015. *Microphis brachyurus* ssp. *lineatus*. *The IUCN Red List of Threatened Species* 2015: e.T46108938A46959096. https://dx.doi.org/10.2305/IUCN.UK.2015-4.RLTS.T46108938A46959096.en. (Viewed 5/13/24)

Price, R. 1966. Caribbean Fishing and Fishermen: A Historical Sketch. *American Anthropologist*, vol. 68, no. 6, pp. 1363–83.

Prouzet, A., P. Christmas. 2021. DORIS , Guinotia dentata (Latreille, 1825), https://doris.ffessm.fr/Especes/Guinotia-dentata-Cirique-de-riviere-1197 (Viewed 5/13/24)

Purtelbaugh C.H., C. W. Martin, M.S. Allen, 2020 Poleward expansion of common snook *Centropomus undecimalis* in the northeastern Gulf of Mexico and future research needs. PLoS; 15(6): e0234083. https://www.ncbi.nlm.nih.gov/pmc/articles/PMC7307751/

Pyron, M., A. Covich, Alan. 2003. Migration Patterns, Densities, and Growth of Neritina punctulata Snails in Rio Espiritu Santo and Rio Mameyes, Northeastern Puerto Rico. Caribbean Journal of Science. 39.

Robertson D.R., J. Van Tassell. 2023. Shorefishes of the Greater Caribbean: online information system. Species *Caranx latus* https://biogeodb.stri.si.edu/caribbean/en/thefishes/species/3641 (viewed 5/8/24)

Robertson, D.R. and J Van Tassell. 2023. Shorefishes of the Greater Caribbean: online information system. Species *Awaous bamana* River goby. https://biogeodb.stri.si.edu/caribbean/en/thefishes/species/4479 (viewed 5/12/24)

Robertson, D.R. and J Van Tassell. 2023. Shorefishes of the Greater Caribbean: online information system. Species Mountain Mullet. https://biogeodb.stri.si.edu/caribbean/en/thefishes/species/785 (Viewed 5/13/24)

Robinson, D., C. Henry, A. Mansingh, Akshai. 2002. Toxicity, Bioaccumulation and Tissue Partitioning of Dieldrin by the Shrimp, Macrobrachium Faustinum de Sassure, in Fresh and Brackish Waters of Jamaica. Environmental technology. 23. 1275-84.

Rodiles-Hernandez, R., A. González-Díaz, C. Chan-Sala, C. 2005. Lista de peces continentales de Chiapas, México. Hidrobiológica: [revista del Departamento de Hidrobiología]. 15. 245-253.

Rodríguez-Almaraz, G.A., E. Campos. 1996. New locality records of freshwater decapods from México (Crustacea: Atyidae, Cambaridae, and Palaemonidae). Proc. Biol. Soc. Wash. 109: 34-38.

Rodríguez-Barreras R., C. Zapata-Arroyo, W. Falcón L. M. De Lourdes Olmeda. 2020. An island invaded by exotics: a review of freshwater fish in Puerto Rico, Neotropical Biodiversity, 6:1, 42-59.

Rueda, P. 2002. Stomach content analysis of Mugil cephalus and Mugil curema (Mugiliformes: Mugilidae) with emphasis on diatoms in the Tamiahua lagoon, México. Revista de biología tropical. 50. 245-52

Schmidt, R., E. McMullin, J. Wright, B. Weatherwax. 2021. Description of larvae of Eleotris perniger (Teleostei: Eleotridae) in transition from saltwater to freshwater from Montserrat, West Indies. Novitates Caribaea (Online). 10.33800/nc.vi18.263. https://novitatescaribaea.do/index.php/novitates/article/view/263/339

Schultz L. P. 1944. A Revision of the American Clingfish, Family Gobiesocidae, with Descriptions of New Genera and Forms. Proceedings of the United States National Museum. 1944 Vol 96, No.3187

Searchlight Newspaper. 18/4/23 EnGenDer project to benefit tri-tri fishers island-wide https://www.searchlight.vc/news/2023/04/18/engender-project-benefit-tri-tri-fishers-island-wide/ (viewed on 5/12/24)

Simmons Associates. 2015. ST. VINCENT AND THE GRENADINES FIFTH NATIONAL REPORT TO THE UNITED NATIONS CONVENTION ON BIOLOGICAL DIVERSITY 2015 https://www.cbd.int/doc/world/vc/vc-nr-05-en.pdf (Viewed 5/13/24)

Simon, M. 2014. Absurd creature of the week. https://www.wired.com/2014/06/absurd-creature-of-the-week-clingfish/ (Viewed 5/22/24)

Smith, W., T. Kwak. 2014. Otolith microchemistry of tropical diadromous fishes: Spatial and migratory dynamics. Journal of fish biology. 84.

Smithsonian Environmental Research Centre. 2012. Melanoides tubercula. https://invasions.si.edu/nemesis/Panama/species_summary/71533#:~:text=Melanoides%20tuberculata%20grazes%20on%20microalgae,2012 (Viewed 5/13/24)

Smith-Vaniz, W.F. 2002. CARANGIDAE. In book: The living marine resources of the Western Central Atlantic. Vol. 2. Bony fishes part 3 (Opistognathidae-Molidae) Edition: FAO Species Identification Guide for Fishery Purposes an American Society of Ichthyologists and Herpetologists Special Publication No. 5. Rome, FAO Chapter: SnooksPublisher: FOOD AND AGRICULTURE ORGANIZATION OF THE UNITED NATIONS Editors: K.E. Carpenter

Snow J.T. 2024. Mexican Fish.com - Burro Grunt https://mexican-fish.com/burro-grunt/#:~:text=The%20Burro%20Grunt%20has%20an,fin%20has%20a%20black%20margin. (Viewed on 5/12/24)

Snow J.T. 2024. Mexican Fish.com – Mountain Mullet. https://mexican-fish.com/mountain-mullet/ (Viewed 5/13/24)

St. Vincent Electricity Services Ltd. (VINLEC) web page. https://www.vinlec.com/contents/operations (Viewed 5/13/24)

St. Vincent Times. Jan 2 1 2024. St Vincent grapples with increased energy use amidst drought concerns https://www.stvincenttimes.com/st-vincent-energy-demand-exceeds-projections/ (Viewed 5/13/240)

Staugler, B. 2019. The Life Cycle of the Common Snook https://blogs.ifas.ufl.edu/charlotteco/2019/06/14/the-life-cycle-of-common-snook/ (viewed 5/9/24)

Tavares, M. 2003 True Crabs. pp. 327-352. In Carpenter, K.E. (ed.) The living marine resources of the Western Central Atlantic. Volume1: introdution, molluscs, crustaceans, hagfishes, sharks, batoid fishes, and chimaeras. FAO Species Identification Guide for Fishery Purposes and American Society of Ichthyologists and Herpetologists Special PublicationNo. 5. Rome, FAO. pp. 1-600.

Torati, L., S. De Grave, T. Page, A. Anker. 2011. Atyidae and Palaemonidae (Crustacea: Decapoda: Caridea) of Bocas del Toro, Panama. Check List. 7.

Valencia, D., M. Campos. 2007. Freshwater Prawns Of The Genus Macrobrachium Bate, 1868 (Crustacea: Decapoda: Palaemonidae) Of Colombia. Zootaxa. 1-44.

Van Meerbeeck, C., F. Zermoglio, A. Roncerel. 2021. OECS CCASAP Country analysis: Resilience to climate change at a glance - Saint Vincent and the Grenadines.

von Hagen, H.O. 1977. The tree-climbing crabs of Trinidad. Studies on the Fauna of Curaçao and other Caribbean Islands, 54(1), 25–59.

Watson, R. E. 2000. Sicydium from the Dominican Republic with description of a new species (Teleostei: Gobiidae). *Stuttgarter Beiträge zur Naturkunde. Serie A (Biologie).* 608: 1-31.

Watson, R.E. 1996. Revision of the subgenus Awaous (Chonophorus) (Teleostei: Gobiidae). Ichthyol. Explor. Freshwat. 7(1):1-18.

Watson, R. E. (2000) Sicydium from the Dominican Republic with description of a new species (Teleostei: Gobiidae). Stuttgarter Beiträge zur Naturkunde. Serie A (Biologie). 608: 1-31.

Wikipedia. 2024. Herbbert Hutingdon Smith. https://en.wikipedia.org/wiki/Herbert_Huntingdon_Smith viewed 27/3/24

Winemiller, K.O., and B.J. Ponwith. 1998. Comparative ecology of eleotrid fishes in Central American coastal streams. Environmental Biology of Fishes 53: 373-384.

Withers, P. Canada proposes shutdown of troubled Maritime elver fishery in 2024. Feb 2024, CBC News. https://www.cbc.ca/news/canada/nova-scotia/canada-proposes-shutdown-of-troubled-maritime-elver-fishery-in-2024-1.7113631   (Viewed 4/30/24)

World Bank Group. 2021. Climate Change Knowledge Portal – St. Vincent and the Grenadines https://climateknowledgeportal.worldbank.org/country/st-vincent-and-grenadines/climate-data-historical (Viewed 25/6/23)

World Health Rankings. 2024. https://www.worldlifeexpectancy.com/saint-vincent-prostate-cancer   (viewed 5/16/24)

APPENDIX 1. TECHNICAL TERMS AND MEASUREMENTS

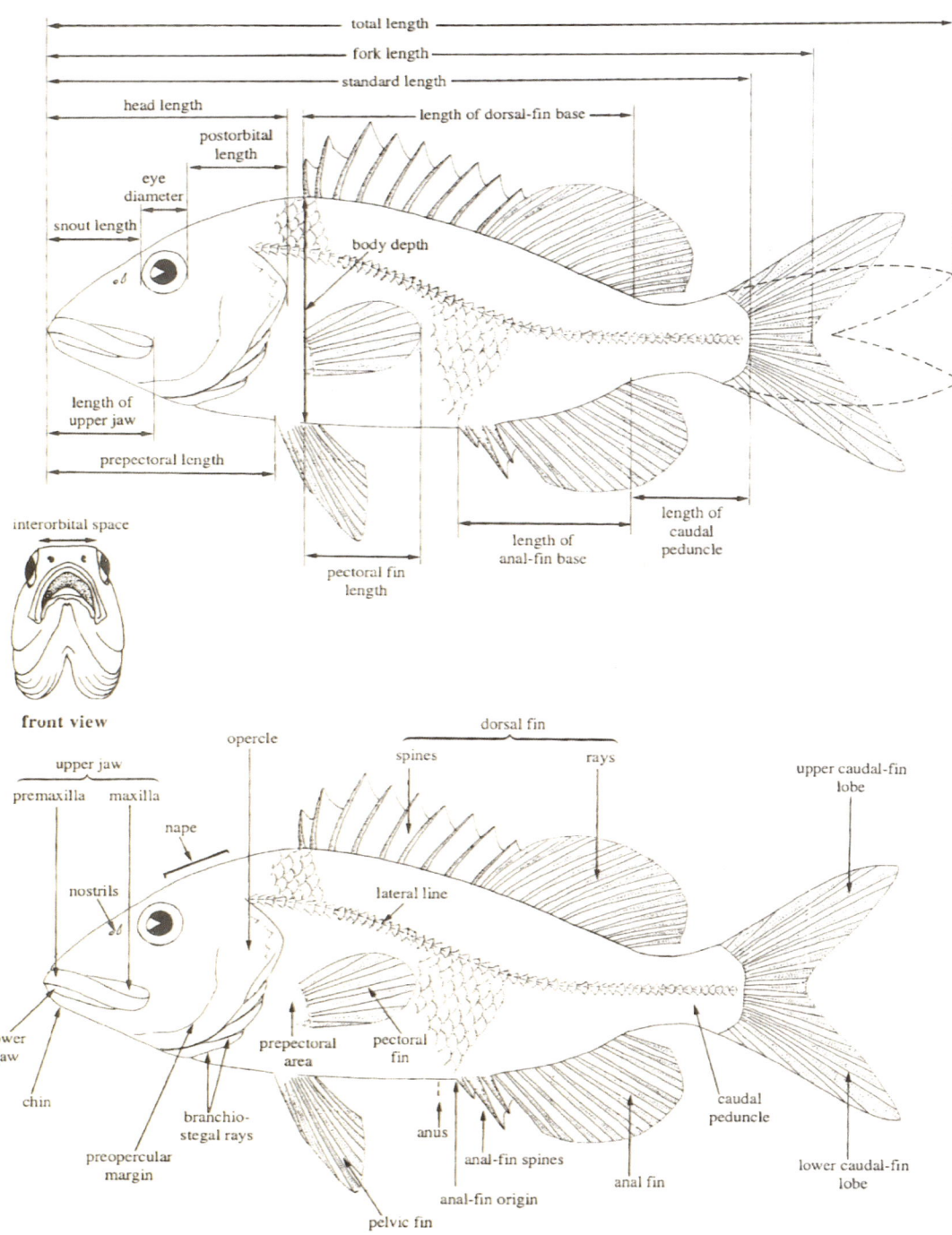

Figure 1. Morpholocical characteristics and measurements of fish taken from Cervigón F R Cipriani, W. Fischer, L. Garibaldi, M.Hendrix, Lemus A.J.,Marquez R, Poutiers J.M., Robaina G., Rodriguez B, 1993 Field Guide to the Commercial Marine and Brackish-Water Resources of the Northern Coast of South America, Food and Agriculture Organisation of the United Nations, Rome.

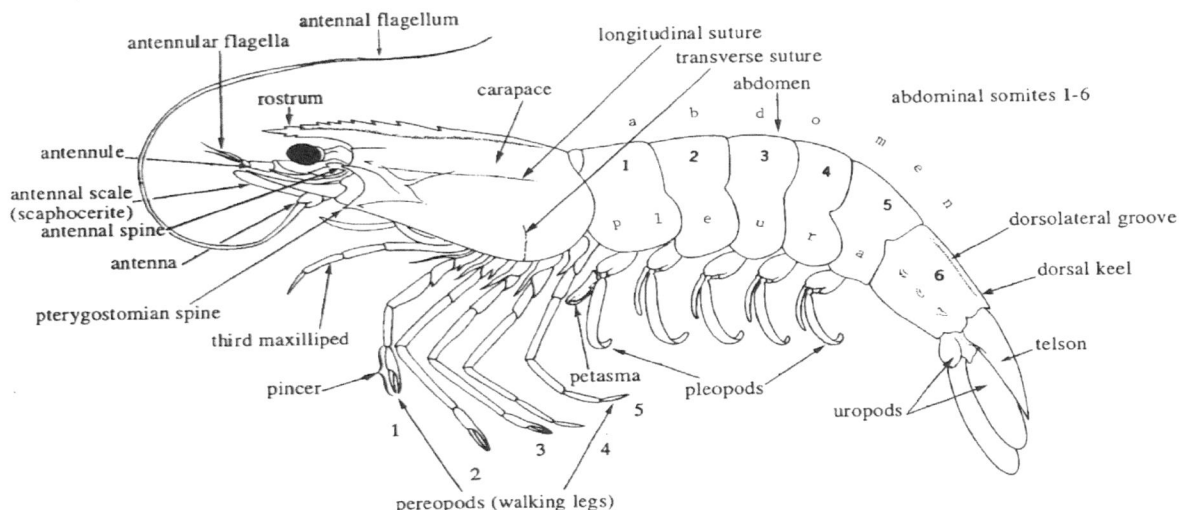

Figure 2. The morphological characteristics of shrimp taken from Cervigón F R Cipriani, W. Fischer, L. Garibaldi, M.Hendrix, Lemus A.J.,Marquez R, Poutiers J.M., Robaina G., Rodriguez B, 1993 Field Guide to the Commercial Marine and Brackish-Water Resources of the Northern Coast of South America, Food and Agriculture Organisation of the United Nations, Rome.

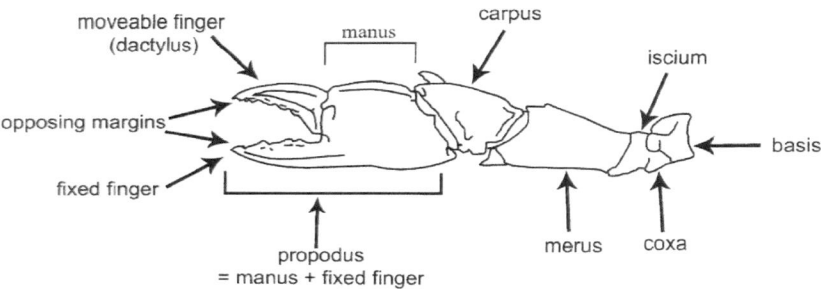

Figure 3. The anatomy of the decapod crustacean cheliped (leg bearing a claw). The above example is a crab cheliped. Taken from Einarsson, Elisabeth & Praszkier, Aron & Vajda, Vivi. (2016). First evidence of the Cretaceous decapod crustacean Protocallianassa from Sweden. Geological Society, London, Special Publications.

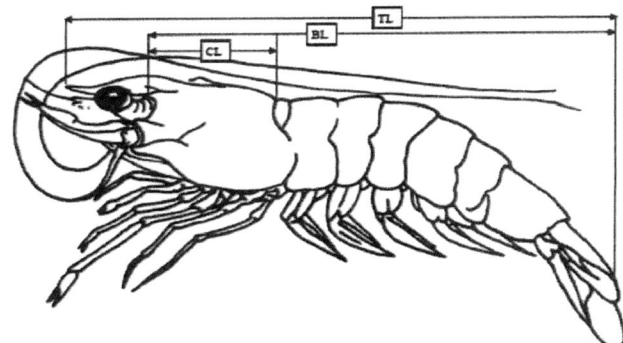

Figure 4. A diagrammatic representation of the morphometric characteristics of shrimp. Total length (TL), body length (BL) and carapace length (CL). Taken From: Badamana, Mohamed & Junga, Joseph & Kaka, Rashid & Ruwa, R. & Karisa, Harrison C. (2019). Morphometric variations among populations of the wild Penaeid shrimps in Malindi–Ungwana Bay along the Northern Coast of Kenya.

APPENDIX 2. RIVER FISHERS' QUESTIONNAIRE

Section 1

Name of Fisher ………………………………………… Age……………………………………………………

Home Address …………………………………………. Phone # ……………………………………………

Name of River and Sections of Rivers Fished e.g. Rutland River (Belle Wood)

……

……

Do you fish to sell?   Yes   Sometimes   Personal Consumption Only
Do you sell crayfish? Yes   Sometimes   Personal Consumption Only

Do you catch river fish to order? Yes No

Do you catch crayfish to order? Yes No

What price do you charge for river fish …………………………crayfish………………………………

river lobster………………………………… crabs……………………………………

Is the sale of river fish and an important part of your income? Big/ Significant/Small

Is the sale of crayfish an important part of your income? Big/Significant/Small

How often do you eat river fish and crayfish?………………………………………………………

Which fish species do you aim to catch?………………………………………………………………

Which crayfish species do you aim to catch? ………………………………………………………

How many people in your village regularly fish in the river?………………………………

Is the number of persons fishing in the river in your area increasing/decreasing /the same?

If there is a change in number of persons fishing and if so why?………………………

……

Are any species no longer found in the areas you fish? ………………………………………

Are river fish and crayfish as plentiful as before? ………………………………………………

Other Notes:

Section 2.

The river fishers were shown photographs of all known freshwater fish, shrimp and crab species and asked the following questions about each.

1. What name do you call this species?

2. Do you fish for this species?

3. How do you catch this species?

4. Is there any time of day or season to fish for this species?

5. Is this species common? Always, abundant, frequent, occasional, rare.

6. What is the river bottom like where this species is found? Big stones, small stones, sand, mud.

7. Where in the river is this species found? Upper, middle or lower sections. Pools, runs, riffles.

8. What cover does this species use? Under banks, deep pools, stones, plants, leaf pack.

www.ingramcontent.com/pod-product-compliance
Lightning Source LLC
LaVergne TN
LVRC080724070526
838199LV00041B/730